Lecture Notes
in Business Information Processing   **382**

More information about this series at http://www.springer.com/series/7911

Sophie Dupuy-Chessa · Henderik A. Proper (Eds.)

Advanced Information Systems Engineering Workshops

CAiSE 2020 International Workshops
Grenoble, France, June 8–12, 2020
Proceedings

 Springer

Editors
Sophie Dupuy-Chessa
LIG
Université Grenoble Alpes
Saint Martin D'Heres, France

Henderik A. Proper (iD)
Luxembourg Institute of Science
and Technology
Esch-sur-Alzette, Luxembourg

ISSN 1865-1348   ISSN 1865-1356   (electronic)
Lecture Notes in Business Information Processing
ISBN 978-3-030-49164-2   ISBN 978-3-030-49165-9   (eBook)
https://doi.org/10.1007/978-3-030-49165-9

This Springer imprint is published by the registered company Springer Nature Switzerland AG
The registered company address is: Gewerbestrasse 11, 6330 Cham, Switzerland

CAISE 2020 Workshops

The International Conference on Advanced Information Systems Engineering (CAiSE), is a well-established and highly visible conference series. It addresses contemporary topics in information systems (IS) engineering such as methodologies and approaches for IS engineering, innovative platforms, architectures, and technologies, as well as engineering of specific kinds of IS. The conference is accompanied by high-quality workshops related to specific information systems engineering topics. They aim at addressing specific emerging challenges, at enabling discussions concerning innovative ideas, as well as at presenting new approaches and tools.

This year the CAiSE conference was planned to be held in Grenoble, France, June 8–12, 2020. Due to the international health context, CAISE 2020 allowed us to experience the conference in a different manner, by being fully virtual. The theme of this 32nd CAiSE conference was particularly well-chosen as it concerns resilient IS, as resilience is a system property that is becoming prominent. Topics included IoT, big data, artificial intelligence, and blockchain or adaptive systems as well as their combination. This year, CAiSE was accompanied by its two long-standing associated working conferences (BPMDS and EMMSAD), as well as seven workshops. The accepted workshops were chosen after careful consideration, based on maturity and compliance with our usual quality and consistency criteria.

In the difficult context, only two workshops were able to adhere to the CAiSE 2020 submission and acceptance guidelines. The paper acceptance rate for these workshops included in this volume was approximately 40% for long papers and 55% for short papers. This volume contains the proceedings of the following two workshops associated with CAiSE 2020:

- The Second International Workshop on Key Enabling Technologies for Digital Factories (KET4DF 2020).
- The First International Workshop on Information Systems Engineering for Smarter Life (ISESL 2020).

The 16th International Workshop on Enterprise & Organizational Modeling and Simulation (EOMAS 2020) published post-proceedings in a separate Springer LNBIP volume.

As workshop chairs of CAiSE 2020 we would like to express our gratitude to all workshop organizers and to all corresponding scientific committees of the workshops for their valuable contribution.

April 2020

Sophie Dupuy-Chessa
Henderik A. Proper

Contents

KET4DF 2020

KET4DF 2020 Preface

The manufacturing industry is entering a new digital era in which ICT technologies and collaboration applications will be integrated with traditional manufacturing practices and processes to increase flexibility and sustainability in manufacturing, mass customization, increase automation, better quality, and improve productivity.

A digital factory is defined as a multi-layered integration of the information related to various activities regarding manufacturing-related resources in the factory and along the product lifecycle. A central aspect of a digital factory to enable stakeholders in the product lifecycle to collaborate using software solutions. The digital factory thus expands outside the actual company boundaries and offers the opportunity for the business and its suppliers to collaborate on business processes that affect the supply chain.

This translates not only into a strong technological evolution but also into an unprecedented extension of companies' information systems. Exploitation of data and services derived from disparate and distributed sources, development of scalable and efficient real-time systems, management of expert knowledge, advanced data analytics, and optimized decision making are some of the key challenges which advanced information systems can address in an effort to reach the vision of Industry 4.0.

The goal of this workshop is to attract high-quality research papers focusing on technologies for Industry 4.0, with specific reference to digital factories and smart manufacturing.

The idea of the workshop was born to promote the research topics of some international projects, which have also become the supporters of the workshop: FIRST (H2020 grant # 734599), UPTIME (H2020 grant # 768634), Z-BRE4K (H2020 grant # 768869), QU4LITY (H2020 grant # 825030), BOOST 4.0 (H2020 grant # 780732), and DIH4CPS (H2020 grant #872548).

The workshop received eight submissions, and the Program Committee selected five high-quality papers for presentation at the workshop, which are included in the CAiSE 2020 workshops proceedings volume.

We thank the workshop chairs of CAiSE 2020, Sophie Dupuy-Chessa and Erik Proper, for their precious support. We also thank the members of the Program Committee and the external reviewers for their hard work in reviewing the submitted papers.

April 2020

Federica Mandreoli
Giacomo Cabri
Gregoris Mentzas
Karl Hribernik

KET4DF 2020 Organization

Organizing Committee

Federica Mandreoli	Università di Modena e Reggio Emilia, Italy
Giacomo Cabri	Università di Modena e Reggio Emilia, Italy
Gregoris Mentzas	ICCS, National Technical University of Athens, Greece
Karl Hribernik	Bremer Institut für Produktion und Logistik GmbH (BIBA), Germany

Program Committee

Marco Aiello	University of Stuttgart, Germany
Kosmas Alexopoulos	University of Patras, Greece
Dimitris Apostolou	University of Piraeus, Greece
Yuewei Bai	Shanghai Polytechnic University, China
Luca Bedogni	Università di Modena e Reggio Emilia, Italy
Alexandros Bousdekis	National Technical University of Athens, Greece
Fabrício Junqueira	University of São Paulo, Brazil
Fenareti Lampathaki	Suite5, Cyprus
Alexander Lazovik	University of Groningen, The Netherlands
Joachim Lentes	Fraunhofer IAO, Germany
Marco Lewandowski	University of Bremen, Germany
Sotirios Makris	University of Patras, Greece
Massimo Mecella	Università Sapienza, Italy
Ifigeneia Metaxa	Atlantis Engineering S.A., Greece
Michele Missikoff	IASI-CNR, Italy
Hervé Panetto	University of Lorraine, France
Pierluigi Petrali	Whirlpool Europe Srl, Italy
Marcos André Pisching	Federal Institute of Santa Catarina, Brazil
Pierluigi Plebani	Politecnico di Milano, Italy
Walter Terkaj	STIIMA-CNR, Italy
Lai Xu	Bournemouth University, UK
Paul de Vrieze	Bournemouth University, UK

Machine Learning for Predictive and Prescriptive Analytics of Operational Data in Smart Manufacturing

Katerina Lepenioti[1], Minas Pertselakis[2], Alexandros Bousdekis[1(✉)],
Andreas Louca[2], Fenareti Lampathaki[2], Dimitris Apostolou[1,3],
Gregoris Mentzas[1], and Stathis Anastasiou[4]

[1] Information Management Unit (IMU), Institute of Communication
and Computer Systems (ICCS), National Technical University
of Athens (NTUA), Athens, Greece
{klepenioti, albous, gmentzas}@mail.ntua.gr
[2] Suite5 Data Intelligence Solutions Limited, Limassol, Cyprus
{minas, andreas, fenareti}@suite5.eu
[3] Department of Informatics, University of Piraeus, Piraeus, Greece
dapost@unipi.gr
[4] M. J. Maillis S.A., Inofyta, Greece
stathis.anastasiou@maillis.com

Abstract. Perceiving information and extracting insights from data is one of the major challenges in smart manufacturing. Real-time data analytics face several challenges in real-life scenarios, while there is a huge treasure of legacy, enterprise and operational data remaining untouched. The current paper exploits the recent advancements of (deep) machine learning for performing predictive and prescriptive analytics on the basis of enterprise and operational data aiming at supporting the operator on the shopfloor. To do this, it implements algorithms, such as Recurrent Neural Networks for predictive analytics, and Multi-Objective Reinforcement Learning for prescriptive analytics. The proposed approach is demonstrated in a predictive maintenance scenario in steel industry.

Keywords: Recurrent Neural Network · Multi-Objective Reinforcement Learning · Deep learning · Industry 4.0 · Predictive maintenance

1 Introduction

Perceiving information and extracting business insights and knowledge from data is one of the major challenges in smart manufacturing [1]. In this sense, advanced data analytics is a crucial enabler of Industry 4.0 [2]. More specifically, among the major challenges for smart manufacturing are: (deep) machine learning, prescriptive analytics in industrial plants, and analytics-based decision support in manufacturing operations [3]. The wide adoption of IoT devices, sensors and actuators in manufacturing environments has fostered an increasing research interest on real-time data analytics. However, these approaches face several challenges in real-life scenarios: (i) They require a large amount of sensor data that already have experienced events (e.g. failures of -ideally- all possible causes); (ii) They require an enormous computational capacity

S. Dupuy-Chessa and H. A. Proper (Eds.): CAiSE 2020 Workshops, LNBIP 382, pp. 5–16, 2020.
https://doi.org/10.1007/978-3-030-49165-9_1

that cannot be supported by existing computational infrastructure of factories; (iii) In most cases, the sensor data involve only a few components of a production line, or a small number of parameters related to each component (e.g. temperature, pressure, vibration), making impossible to capture the whole picture of the factory shop floor and the possible correlations among all the machines; (iv) The cold-start problem is rarely investigated. On the other hand, there is a huge treasure of legacy, enterprise and operational systems data remaining untouched. Manufacturers are sitting on a goldmine of unexplored historical, legacy and operational data from their Manufacturing Execution Systems (MES), Enterprise Resource Planning systems (ERP), etc. and they cannot afford to miss out on its unexplored potential. However, only 20–30% of the value from such available data-at-rest is currently accrued [4].

Legacy data contain information regarding the whole factory cycle and store events from all machines, whether they have sensors installed or not (e.g. products per day, interruption times of production line, maintenance logs, causalities, etc.) [5]. Therefore, legacy data analytics have the credentials to move beyond KPIs calculations of business reports (e.g. OEE, uptime, etc.), towards providing an all-around view of manufacturing operations on the shopfloor in a proactive manner. In this direction, the recent advancements of machine learning can have a substantial contribution in performing predictive and prescriptive analytics on the basis of enterprise and operational data aiming at supporting the operator on the shopfloor and at extracting meaningful insights. Combining predictive and prescriptive analytics is essential for smarter decisions in manufacturing [2]. In addition mobile computing (with the use of mobile devices, such as smartphones and tablets) can significantly enable timely, comfortable, non-intrusive and reliable interaction with the operator on the shopfloor [6], e.g. for generating alerts, guiding their work, etc. through dedicated mobile apps.

The current paper proposes an approach for predictive and prescriptive analytics on the basis of enterprise and operational data for smart manufacturing. To do this, it develops algorithms based on Recurrent Neural Networks (RNN) for predictive analytics, and Multi-Objective Reinforcement Learning (MORL) for prescriptive analytics. The rest of the paper is organized as follows: Sect. 2 presents the background, the challenges and prominent methods for predictive and prescriptive analytics of enterprise and operational data for smart manufacturing. Section 3 describes the proposed approach, while Sect. 4 shows a walkthrough scenario of the proposed approach in the steel industry. Section 5 presents the experimental results, while Sect. 6 concludes the paper and outlines the plans for future research.

2 Background, Existing Challenges and Novel Methods

2.1 Predictive Analytics for Smart Manufacturing

Background. Intelligent and automated data analysis which aims to discover useful insights from data has become a best practice for modern factories. It is supported today by many software tools and data warehouses, and it is known by the name "descriptive analytics". A step further, however, is to use the same data to feed models that can make predictions with similar or better accuracy than a human expert. In the framework of smart manufacturing, prognostics related to machines' health status is a critical research domain that often leverages machine learning methods and data mining tools. In most of the cases, this is related to the analysis of streaming sensor data mainly for health monitoring [7–9], but also for failure prediction [10–12] as part of a predictive maintenance strategy. However, in all of these approaches, the prediction is produced only minutes or even seconds before the actual failure, which, is not often a realistic and practical solution for a real industrial case. The factory managers need to have this information hours or days before the event, so that there is enough time for them to act proactively and prevent it. One way to achieve this is to perform data mining on maintenance and operational data that capture the daily life-cycle of the shop floor in order to make more high-level predictions [13–15].

Existing Challenges. The most notable challenges related to predictive analytics for smart manufacturing include: (a) Predictions always involve a degree of uncertainty, especially when the data available are not sufficient quantity-wise or quality-wise; (b) Inconsistent, incomplete or missing data with low dimensionality often result into overfitting or underfitting that can lead to misleading conclusions; (c) Properly preparing and manipulating the data in order to conclude to the most appropriate set of features to be used as input to the model is the most time-consuming, yet critical to the accuracy of the algorithms, activity; (d) Lack of a common "language" between data scientists and domain experts hinders the extraction of appropriate hypothesis from the beginning and the correct interpretation and explainability of results.

Novel Methods. *Time series forecasting* involves prediction models that analyze time series data and usually infer future data trends. A time series is a sequence of data points indexed in time order. Unlike regression predictive modeling, time series also adds the complexity of a sequence dependence among the input variables. *Recurrent Neural Networks (RNN)* are considered to be powerful neural networks designed to handle sequence dependence. *Long Short-Term Memory Network (LSTM)* is a type of RNN that is typically used in deep learning for its ability to learn long-term dependencies and handle multiple input and output variables.

2.2   Prescriptive Analytics for Smart Manufacturing

Background. Prescriptive analytics aims at answering the questions "What should I do?" and "Why should I do it?". It is able to bring business value through adaptive, time-dependent and optimal decisions on the basis of predictions about future events [16]. During the last years, there is an increasing interest on prescriptive analytics for smart manufacturing [17], and is considered to be the next evolutionary step towards increasing data analytics maturity for optimized decision making, ahead of time.

Existing Challenges. The most important challenges of prescriptive analytics include [2, 17, 18]: (i) Addressing the uncertainty introduced by the predictions, the incomplete and noisy data and the subjectivity in human judgement; (ii) Combining the "learned knowledge" of machine learning and data mining methods with the "engineered knowledge" elicited from domain experts; (iii) Developing generic prescriptive analytics methods and algorithms utilizing artificial intelligence and machine learning instead of problem-specific optimization models; (iv) Incorporating adaptation mechanisms capable of processing data and human feedback to continuously improve decision making process over time and to generate non-intrusive prescriptions; (v) Recommending optimal plans out of a list of alternative (sets of) actions.

Novel Methods. *Reinforcement Learning (RL)* is considered to be a third machine learning paradigm, alongside supervised learning and unsupervised learning [19]. RL shows an increasing trend in research literature as a tool for optimal policies in manufacturing problems (e.g. [20, 21]). In RL, the problem is represented by an environment consisting of states and actions and learning agents with a defined goal state. The agents aim to reach the goal state while maximizing the rewards by selecting actions and moving to different states. In *Interactive RL*, there is the additional capability of incorporating evaluative feedback by a human observer so that the RL agent learns from both human feedback and environmental reward [22]. Another extension is *Multi-Objective RL (MORL)*, which is a sequential decision making problem with multiple objectives. MORL requires a learning agent to obtain action policies that can optimize multiple objectives at the same time [23].

3 The Proposed Approach

The proposed approach consists of a predictive analytics component (Sect. 3.1) and a prescriptive analytics component (Sect. 3.2) that process enterprise and operational data from manufacturing legacy systems, as depicted in Fig. 1. The communication is conducted through an event broker for the event predictions and the actions prescriptions, while other parameters (i.e. objective values and alternative actions) become available through RESTful APIs. The results are communicated to business users and shopfloor operators through intuitive interfaces addressed to both computers and mobile devices.

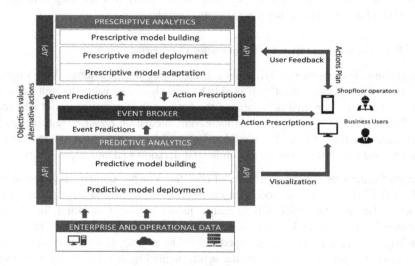

Fig. 1. The architecture of the proposed approach.

3.1 Recurrent Neural Network for Predictive Analytics

The proposed predictive analytics approach aims to: (i) exploit hidden correlations inside the data that derive from the day-to-day shop floor operations, (ii) create and adjust a predictive model able to identify future machinery failures, and (iii) make estimations regarding the *timing* of the failure, i.e. when a failure of the machinery may occur, given the history of operations on the factory. This type of data usually contains daily characteristics that derive from the production line operations and are typically collected as part of a world-wide best practice for monitoring, evaluation and improvement of the effectiveness of the production process. The basic measurement of this process is an industry standard known as Overall Equipment Effectiveness (OEE) and is computed as: OEE(%) = Availability(%) × Performance(%) × Quality (%). Availability is the ratio of actual operational time versus the planned operational time, Performance is the ratio of actual throughput of products versus the maximum potential throughput, and the Quality is the ratio of the not-rejected items produced vs the total production. The OEE factor can be computed for the whole production line as an indication of the factory's effectiveness or per machine or a group of machines. The proposed methodology takes advantage of these commonly extracted indicators and processes them in two steps: in predictive model building (learning) and predictive model deployment.

Predictive Model Building. The predictive analytics model incorporates LSTM and exploits its unique ability to "remember" a sequence of patterns and its relative insensitivity to possible time gaps in the time series. As in most neural network algorithms, LSTM networks are able to seamlessly model non-linear problems with multiple input variables through the iterative training of their parameters (weights). Since the predictive analytics model deals with time-series, the LSTM model is trained using supervised learning on a set of training sequences assigned to a known output value. Therefore, an analyst feeds the model with a set of daily features for a given machine (e.g. the factors that produce the OEE) and use as outcome the number of days until the next failure. This number is known since historical data can hold this information. Nevertheless, when the model is finally built and put in operation, it will use new input data and will have to estimate the new outcome.

Predictive Model Deployment. When the LSTM model is fed with new data it can produce an estimation of when the next failure will occur (i.e. number of days or hours) and what is the expected interruption duration in the following days. Although this estimation may not be 100% accurate, it could help factory managers to program maintenance actions proactively in a flexible and dynamic manner, compared to an often rigid and outdated schedule that is currently the common practice. This estimation feeds into prescriptive analytics aiming at automating the whole decision-making process and provide optimal plans.

3.2 Multi-Objective Reinforcement Learning for Prescriptive Analytics

The proposed prescriptive analytics approach is able to: (i) recommend (prescribe) both perfect and imperfect actions (e.g. maintenance actions with various degrees of restoration); (ii) model the decision making process under uncertainty instead of the physical manufacturing process, thus making it applicable to various industries and production processes; and, (iii) incorporate the preference of the domain expert into the decision making process (e.g. according to their skills, experience, etc.), in the form of feedback over the generated prescriptions. To do these, it incorporates Multi-Objective Reinforcement Learning (MORL). Unlike most of the Multi-objective Optimization approaches which result in the Pareto front set of optimal solutions [24], the proposed approach provides a single optimal solution (prescription), thus generating more concrete insights to the user. The proposed prescriptive analytics algorithm consists of three steps: prescriptive model building, prescriptive model solving, and prescriptive model adapting, which are described in detail below.

Prescriptive Model Building. The prescriptive analytics model representing the decision making process is defined by a tuple (S, A, T, R), where S is the state space, A is the action space, T is the transition function $T : S \times A \times S \rightarrow \mathbb{R}$ and R is the vector reward function $R : S \times A \times S \rightarrow \mathbb{R}^n$ where the n-dimensions are associated with the objectives to be optimized O_n. The proposed prescriptive analytics model has a single starting state S_N, from which the agent starts the episode, and a state S_B that the agent tries to avoid. Each episode of the training process of the RL agent will end, when the agent returns to the normal state S_N or when it reaches S_B. Figure 2 depicts an example including 3 alternative (perfect and/or imperfect maintenance) actions (or sets of actions) $S_{A_i}, i = 1, 2, 3$, each one of which is assigned to a reward vector. The prescriptive analytics model is built dynamically. In this sense, the latest updates on the number of the action states S_{A_i} and the estimations of the objectives' values for each state S_k are retrieved through APIs from the predictive analytics. Each action may be implemented either before the breakdown (in order to eliminate or mitigate its impact) or after the breakdown (if this occurs before the implementation of mitigating actions). After the implementation of each action, the equipment returns to its normal state S_N. Solid lines represent the transitions a_i that have non-zero reward with respect to the optimization objectives and move the agent from one state to another.

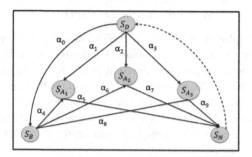

Fig. 2. An example of the prescriptive analytics model with 3 alternative (sets of) actions.

Prescriptive Model Deployment. On the basis of event triggers for predicted abnormal situations (e.g. about the time of the next breakdown) received through a message broker, the model moves from the normal state S_N to the dangerous state S_D. For each objective, the reward functions are defined according to whether the objective is to be maximized or minimized. On this basis, the optimal policy $\pi_{O_i}(s, a)$, for each objective O_i is calculated with the use of the actor-critic algorithm, which is a policy gradient algorithm aiming at searching directly in (some subset of) the policy space starting with a mapping from a finite-dimensional (parameter) space to the space of policies [23]. Assuming independent objectives, the multi-objective optimal policy is derived from: $\pi_{opt}(s, a) = \prod_{i \in I} \pi_{O_i}(s, a)$. The time constraints of the optimal policy (prescription) are defined by the prediction event trigger. The prescription is exposed to the operator on the shop-floor (e.g. through a mobile device) providing them the capability to accept or reject it. If accepted, the prescribed action is added to the actions plan.

Prescriptive Model Adaptation. The prescriptive analytics model is able to adapt according to feedback by the expert over the generated prescriptions. This approach learns from the operator whether the prescribed actions converge with their experience or skills and incorporates their preference to the prescriptive analytics model. In this way, it provides non-disruptive decision augmentation and thus, achieves an optimized human-machine interaction, while, at the same time, optimizing manufacturing KPIs. To do this, it implements the policy shaping algorithm [25], a Bayesian approach that attempts to maximize the information gained from human feedback by utilizing it as direct labels on the policy. For each prescription, optional human feedback is received as a signal of approval or rejection, numerically mapped to the reward signals and interpreted into a step function. The feedback is converted into a policy $\pi_{feedback}(s, a)$, the distribution of which relies on the consistency, expressing the user's knowledge regarding the optimality of the actions, and the likelihood of receiving feedback. Assuming that the feedback policy is independent from the optimal multi-objective policy, the synthetic optimal policy for the optimization objectives and the human feedback is calculated as: $\pi_{opt}(s, a) = \pi_{opt}(s, a) * \pi_{feedback}(s, a)$.

4 A Predictive Maintenance Scenario in the Steel Industry

The case examined is the cold rolling production line of M. J. Maillis S.A. Cold rolling is a process of reduction of the cross-sectional area through the deformation caused by a pair of rotating in opposite directions metal rolls in order to produce rolling products with the closest possible thickness tolerances and an excellent surface finish. In the milling station, there is one pair of back up rolls and one pair of work rolls. The deformation takes place through force of the rolls supported by adjustable strip tension in both coilers and de-coilers. Over the life of the roll some wear will occur due to normal processing, and some wear will occur due to extraneous conditions. During replacement, the rolls are removed for grinding, during which some roll diameter is lost, and then are stored in the warehouse for future use. After several regrinding, the diameter of the roll becomes so small that is no longer operational.

The LSTM model of predictive analytics was created using the Keras library with Tensorflow as backend and the MORL using Brown-UMBC Reinforcement Learning and Planning (BURLAP) library, while the event communication between them is performed with a Kafka broker. In the M. J. Maillis S.A case, the system predicts the time of the next breakdown and the RUL of the available rolls. For the latter, the operator can select one of the repaired rollers, having been subject to grinding, or a new one. Therefore, the alternative actions are created dynamically according to the available repaired rollers existing in the warehouse. Each one has a different RUL, according to its previous operation, and a different cost (retrieved from enterprise systems) due to its depreciation. Each roller has an ID and is assigned to its characteristics/objectives of MORL (i.e. cost to be minimized and RUL to be maximized) in order to facilitate its traceability. The available rolls along with the aforementioned objectives values are retrieved on the basis of a predicted breakdown event trigger.

Table 1. The alternative actions, their costs and their RULs.

Actions	Cost *(Euro)*	RUL *(days)*
Replace with new roller	8,000	12
Replace with repaired roller ID1	5,284	5
Replace with repaired roller ID2	3,510	4
Replace with repaired roller ID3	4,831	6

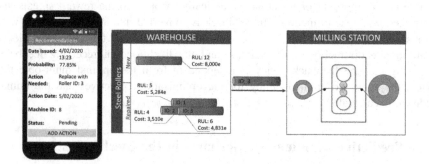

Fig. 3. Illustration of the scenario under examination.

The alternative actions for the current scenario along with their costs and RULs are shown in Table 1. The action "Replace with new roller" represents a perfect maintenance action, while the rest ones represent imperfect maintenance actions. Figure 3 depicts an example of the process in which the prescription "Replace with repaired roller ID3" is generated on the basis of a breakdown prediction and previously received feedback and instantly communicated to the operators through a dedicated mobile app. The operators are also expected to provide feedback so that their knowledge and preferences are incorporated in the system and the models are adapted accordingly.

5 Experimental Results

5.1 Evaluation of the Predictions About the Timing of Interruptions

The legacy datasets used are related to the OEE of M. J. Maillis S.A. factory for the years 2017, 2018 and 2019. The datasets included a total of 21 features and some of the most useful were the real operational time, the time of interruptions and the duration of the breakdown events. A multivariate time series model was designed, as several input features were used in order to predict one output feature. To this direction, the first time series analysis performed in order to predict when the next interruption will occur ('*When do we expect the next interruption?*'). A new feature named 'Days from next breakdown event' was created, and the model was trained. The input features selected for this prediction were: Availability, Performance, Minutes of Breakdown, Minutes of Interruptions, Real Gross Production and the date. After preprocessing the data, the appropriate sequences were extracted that would allow for several timesteps to be selected and tested for the analysis. In our case, timestep represented the last "n" days that the model will use. The LSTM model was then created by testing several layers, optimizers, neurons, batch sizes and epochs until the best performing model was designed. The final result ended being a sequential model with a first LSTM layer of 32 neurons, a second LSTM layer of 16 neurons, a dropout layer with rate 0.1, and finally a dense layer. The model was then trained using data from 2017, 2018 and six months of 2019; with an rmsprop optimizer, a batch size of 1, a timestep of 1, an epochs value of 300, and an early stopping that reached the best performance around 100 epochs. Predictions deal with the last six months of 2019, and the result can be seen in Fig. 4. The blue line represents the actual values and the orange line represents the predicted values. The RMSE came to be 1.26, meaning that there is an average of 1.26 days uncertainty in every result predicted.

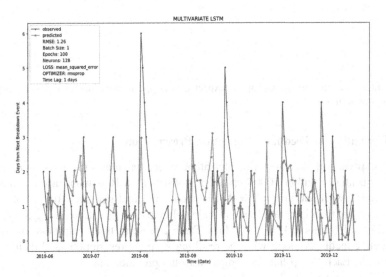

Fig. 4. LSTM result - prediction of when the next interruption will occur. (Color figure online)

5.2   Evaluation of the Predictions About the Duration of Interruptions

The second analysis aimed to predict the expected interruption duration for the following day ('*Which is the expected interruption duration for the following day?*'). The input features used in this LSTM model were: Availability, Performance, Minutes of breakdown, Real Gross Production, Number of breakdowns, and month (date). Again, several LSTM parameters and layers were tested and the final model resulted to be a sequential model with a first LSTM layer of 24 neurons and an activation function 'relu', a second layer of 12 neurons with a 'relu' activation function, a dropout layer of 0.1 rate, and finally a dense layer. The model was trained using data from 2017 and 2018; using a batch size of 20, 100 epochs, a timestep of 3 and an rmsprop optimizer. Predictions were performed in 2019 data and results are depicted in Fig. 5. The blue line represents the actual value whereas the orange line represents the predicted value. The overall RMSE is 107.57, meaning that there is an average of 107.57 min uncertainty in each prediction.

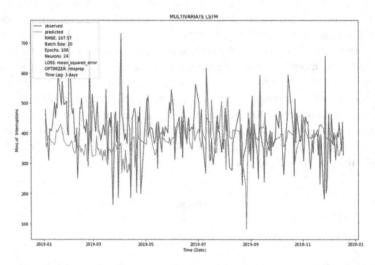

Fig. 5. LSTM result - prediction of the expected interruption duration for the following day. (Color figure online)

5.3   Evaluation of Feedback Impact on Prescriptions

For this experiment, the actor-critic algorithm, which calculates the associated optimal policy sequentially within 10000 episodes, consists of a Boltzmann actor and a TD-Lambda critic with learning rate = 0.3, lambda = 0.4 and gamma = 0.99. The generated policies are then integrated into a single policy taking into account the consistency (C = 0.7) and likelihood (L = 0.8) values. Table 2 presents five "snapshots" of positive and negative feedback along with the resulting shaped prescriptions and their respective policies. Each "snapshot" is compared to the previous one.

Table 2. Evaluation of feedback impact on prescriptive analytics.

#	Initial prescription	Initial policy	Positive feedback	Negative feedback	Shaped prescription	Shaped policy
1	ID2	0.998900	5	7	ID2	0.155000
2	ID2	0.155000	5	12	ID2	0.000410
3	ID2	0.000410	5	18	ID3	0.000075
4	ID3	0.000075	7	14	ID1	0.000022
5	ID1	0.000022	0	4	New roller	0.000004

6 Conclusion and Future Work

In this paper, we proposed an approach for predictive and prescriptive analytics aiming at exploiting the huge treasure of legacy enterprise and operational data and to overcome some challenges of real-time data analytics. The potential of the proposed approach is high, especially in traditional industries that have not benefit from the advancements of Industry 4.0 and that have just started investigating the potential of data analytics and machine learning for the optimization of their production processes. The traditional manufacturing sectors (e.g. textile, furniture, packaging, steel processing) have usually older factories with limited capacity on investing in modern production technologies. Since the neural networks are inherently adaptive, the proposed approach could be applied to similar production lines (e.g. at a newly established factory of the same type) overcoming the cold-start problem, due to which other techniques usually fail. It also exploits both the "voice of data" and the "voice of experts". Regarding future work, we plan to evaluate our proposed approach in additional use cases, with different requirements, as well as to investigate approaches and algorithms for fusion of the outcomes derived from real-time data analytics and operational data analytics that represent different levels of information.

Acknowledgments. This work is funded by the European Commission project H2020 UPTIME "Unified Predictive Maintenance System" (768634).

References

1. Gröger, C.: Building an industry 4.0 analytics platform. Datenbank Spektrum **18**, 5–14 (2018). https://doi.org/10.1007/s13222-018-0273-1
2. Menezes, B., Kelly, J., Leal, A., Le Roux, G.: Predictive, prescriptive and detective analytics for smart manufacturing in the information age. IFAC-PapersOnLine **52**, 568–573 (2019)
3. Big Data Challenges in Smart Manufacturing: A discussion paper for BDVA and EFFRA Research & Innovation roadmap alignment BDVA. http://www.bdva.eu/node/1002
4. The age of analytics: competing in a data-driven world. https://www.mckinsey.com/business-functions/mckinsey-analytics/our-insights/the-age-of-analytics-competing-in-a-data-driven-world
5. Pertselakis, M., Lampathaki, F., Petrali, P.: Predictive maintenance in a digital factory shop-floor: data mining on historical and operational data coming from manufacturers' information systems. In: Proper, H., Stirna, J. (eds.) Advanced Information Systems

Engineering Workshops. LNBIP, vol. 349, pp. 120–131. Springer, Cham (2019). https://doi. org/10.1007/978-3-030-20948-3_11

6. Yang, H., Kumara, S., Bukkapatnam, S., Tsung, F.: The internet of things for smart manufacturing: a review. IISE Trans. **51**, 1190–1216 (2019)

7. Lee, J., Lapira, E., Bagheri, B., Kao, H.: Recent advances and trends in predictive manufacturing systems in big data environment. Manuf. Lett. **1**, 38–41 (2013)

8. Kobbacy, K., Fawzi, B., Percy, D., Ascher, H.: A full history proportional hazards model for preventive maintenance scheduling. Qual. Reliab. Eng. Int. **13**, 187–198 (1997)

9. Lin, C., Tseng, H.: A neural network application for reliability modelling and condition-based predictive maintenance. Int. J. Adv. Manuf. Technol. **25**, 174–179 (2004)

10. Choudhary, A., Harding, J., Tiwari, M.: Data mining in manufacturing: a review based on the kind of knowledge. J. Intell. Manuf. **20**, 501–521 (2008)

11. Harding, J., Shahbaz, M., Kusiak, A.S.: Data mining in manufacturing: a review. J. Manuf. Sci. Eng. **128**, 969–976 (2005)

12. Bey-Temsamani, A., Engels, M., Motten, A., Vandenplas, S., Ompusunggu, A.P.: A practical approach to combine data mining and prognostics for improved predictive maintenance. In: The Data Mining Case Studies Workshop (DMCS), 15th ACM SIGKDD Conference on Knowledge Discovery and Data Mining (KDD 2009), Paris, pp. 37–44 (2009)

13. Bastos, P., Lopes, I., Pires, L.C.M.: Application of data mining in a maintenance system for failure prediction. In: Safety, Reliability and Risk Analysis: Beyond the Horizon: 22nd European Safety and Reliability, vol. 1, pp. 933–940 (2014)

14. Romanowski, C.J., Nagi, R.: Analyzing maintenance data using data mining methods. In: Braha, D. (ed.) Data Mining for Design and Manufacturing. MACO, vol. 3, pp. 235–254. Springer, Boston (2001). https://doi.org/10.1007/978-1-4757-4911-3_10

15. Susto, G., Schirru, A., Pampuri, S., McLoone, S., Beghi, A.: Machine learning for predictive maintenance: a multiple classifier approach. IEEE Trans. Ind. Inf. **11**, 812–820 (2015)

16. Šikšnys, L., Pedersen, T.B.: Prescriptive analytics. In: Liu, L., Özsu, M. (eds.) Encyclopedia of Database Systems. Springer, New York (2016). https://doi.org/10.1007/978-1-4899-7993-3

17. Vater, J., Harscheidt, L., Knoll, A.: Smart manufacturing with prescriptive analytics. In: 2019 8th International Conference on Industrial Technology and Management (ICITM), pp. 224–228. IEEE (2019)

18. Lepenioti, K., Bousdekis, A., Apostolou, D., Mentzas, G.: Prescriptive analytics: literature review and research challenges. Int. J. Inf. Manag. **50**, 57–70 (2020)

19. Sutton, R., Barto, A.G.: Reinforcement Learning: An Introduction. MIT Press, Cambridge (2018)

20. Dornheim, J., Link, N., Gumbsch, P.: Model-free adaptive optimal control of episodic fixed-horizon manufacturing processes using reinforcement learning. Int. J. Control Autom. Syst. (2019). https://doi.org/10.1007/s12555-019-0120-7

21. Rocchetta, R., Bellani, L., Compare, M., Zio, E., Patelli, E.: A reinforcement learning framework for optimal operation and maintenance of power grids. Appl. Energy **241**, 291–301 (2019)

22. Li, G., Gomez, R., Nakamura, K., He, B.: Human-centered reinforcement learning: a survey. IEEE Trans. Hum. Mach. Syst. **49**, 337–349 (2019)

23. Liu, C., Xu, X., Hu, D.: Multiobjective reinforcement learning: a comprehensive overview. IEEE Trans. Syst. Man Cybern. Syst. **45**, 385–398 (2015)

24. Tozer, B., Mazzuchi, T., Sarkani, S.: Many-objective stochastic path finding using reinforcement learning. Expert Syst. Appl. **72**, 371–382 (2017)

25. Griffith, S., Subramanian, K., Scholz, J., Isbell, C., Thomaz, A.L.: Policy shaping: integrating human feedback with reinforcement learning. In: NIPS (2013)

Towards Predictive Maintenance for Flexible Manufacturing Using FIWARE

Go Muan Sang[1], Lai Xu[1], Paul de Vrieze[1(✉)], and Yuewei Bai[2]

[1] Faculty of Science and Technology, Bournemouth University,
Poole, Dorset, UK
{gsang, lxu, pdevrieze}@bournemouth.ac.uk
[2] Industry Engineering of Engineering College,
Shanghai Polytechnic University, Shanghai, China
ywbai@sspu.edu.cn

Abstract. Industry 4.0 has shifted the manufacturing related processes from conventional processes within one organization to collaborative processes across different organizations. For example, product design processes, manufacturing processes, and maintenance processes across different factories and enterprises. This complex and competitive collaboration requires the underlying system architecture and platform to be flexible and extensible to support the demands of dynamic collaborations as well as advanced functionalities such as big data analytics. Both operation and condition of the production equipment are critical to the whole manufacturing process. Failures of any machine tools can easily have impact on the subsequent value-added processes of the collaboration. Predictive maintenance provides a detailed examination of the detection, location and diagnosis of faults in related machineries using various analyses. In this context, this paper explores how the FIWARE framework supports predictive maintenance. Specifically, it looks at applying a data driven approach to the Long Short-Term Memory Network (LSTM) model for machine condition and remaining useful life to support predictive maintenance using FIWARE framework in a modular fashion.

Keywords: Predictive maintenance · FIWARE · LSTM · Big data analytics · Industry 4.0

1 Introduction

Modern complex and competitive manufacturing demand flexible and modular systems to optimize production processes; maintenance and market demands; and to support collaborative partners [1, 2]. In the context of Industry 4.0, utilizing emerging technologies such as Internet of things, advanced data analytics and cloud computing provides new opportunities for flexible collaborations as well as effective optimization of manufacturing related processes, e.g. predictive maintenance [1].

Both operation and condition of the production equipment are critical to the whole manufacturing process [3, 5]. Failures of the machine tools easily can have impact such as delay on the subsequent value-added processes of the organization, partners and its customers, due to the interlinked nature of production systems [4, 5]. Essentially, any

© Springer Nature Switzerland AG 2020
S. Dupuy-Chessa and H. A. Proper (Eds.): CAiSE 2020 Workshops, LNBIP 382, pp. 17–28, 2020.
https://doi.org/10.1007/978-3-030-49165-9_2

unplanned failure or inefficient process of manufacturing equipment can result in an unplanned downtime and costs for an entire production line [3, 5]. Traditional processes dealing with maintenance are complex, and costly [6]. It is impossible for the traditional data processing approaches and tools to produce meaningful information from the huge volume of data generated by modern manufacturing processes [7].

Condition-based maintenance utilizes condition measurements to schedule appropriate maintenance activities while minimizing impact to normal machine operations [3, 5]. In order to achieve optimal maintenance decision making, a new approach should be in place to utilize multiple data sources from different data domains. Typically, production data, machine operation and function data, and sensor data are all required for the analysis (real-time, off-line) and used to build models for predicting machine condition i.e. failure, worn, etc., or inefficient process or poor product quality reducing failure times and costs [3, 5, 6]. Real-time monitoring of machine tools and equipment together with predictive models, visualization and data analysis supported by flexible predictive maintenance platform can lead to effective maintenance.

This paper presents an approach for data driven predictive maintenance of machine equipment, based on real-time shop floor monitoring and enhances the collaboration between parties involved through flexible maintenance platform in the context of Industry 4.0 by applying FIWARE framework, enabling modularizing of related functions. The contributions of this work are a) design a predictive maintenance analytics platform based on FIWARE b) propose data-driven approach with Long Short-Term Memory (LSTM) network for RUL estimation, which can make full use of the sensor sequence data, and c) using the design predictive maintenance platform to present the application case.

2   Related Work

The emerging Industry 4.0 drives the focus of modern industrial collaborative computing [1]. Industry 4.0 can be realized as the flexibility that exists in value-creating networks is increased by the application of emerging technologies such as the internet of things, Cyber Physical Systems (CPS), cloud computing, enabling machines and plants to adapt their behaviors to changing orders and operating conditions through self-optimization and reconfiguration [1]. Essentially the data exchanged and produced in such interaction among several components establishes the underlying business processes for collaboration. Collaborative business processes are required being moved across factories and enterprises to effectively manage and ease the life cycle of production and its demands [8, 9]. This requires a flexible and modular platform. Furthermore, with the demand for data to flow across different collaborative domains, new important challenge like transparency and traceability arise [4].

Effective maintenance is essential to decreasing the costs associated with downtime and faulty products in highly competitive and complex manufacturing industries [3, 4]. In the context of predictive maintenance, remaining useful life (RUL) estimation and detecting the tool condition of an equipment enable to schedule effective schedule plan in advance, avoiding unexpected failure, ensuring smooth replacement maintenance, cancelling unnecessary maintenance to reduce cost and adjusting the operating conditions, such as speed, load, to prolong the life of the equipment [3, 5, 6]. RUL of a component or a system is defined as the length from the current time to the end of the useful life whereas tool condition can be described as degradation (worn-out) or health of machine equipment [5, 6, 10].

The condition and health of the production machine is critical to the whole manufacturing process [3–5]. To support this, traditional maintenance approaches such as manual and fixed maintenance scheduling are typically carried out [3]. However, this approach is cumbersome, costly and introduces the possibility of human error [5, 6]. The continuous collection of large amounts of data from sources such as sensors and equipment usage can provide new opportunities to operations and maintenance process to be proactive with ongoing equipment maintenance and upkeep [3, 5]. This enables optimization of the operation and condition of the equipment as well as predict future potential issues in a system or equipment and, therefore utilize maintenance in a predictive manner [3, 5].

Data-driven with machine learning approaches are recognized in providing the rising effective solutions in facilitating the decision-making process, assisted by the advanced capabilities of cloud computing, big data and analytics [7]. There however exist challenges in predictive maintenance; the complexity and the capacity to manage big data with the nature of being dynamic and complex associations, and the flexibility and interoperability to integrate different systems/components [2, 5, 9]. Several conceptual frameworks for predictive maintenance have been proposed in the research community [11–14]. However, key factors such as modular design i.e. to act easily and dynamically based on needs, advanced analytics and middleware capability based on the context of Industry 4.0 standards, are still overlooked. In order to achieve a flexible predictive maintenance with an optimal maintenance decision making, a new approach should be in place to support the integration of different components, multiple data sources from different data domains as well as advanced analytics capabilities in a modular fashion.

3 Predictive Maintenance

3.1 FIWARE Architecture

FIWARE is an open source platform for building smart solutions in different application domains [15]. It offers a catalogue library of components known as Generic Enablers (GEs), along with a set of reference implementations that allow the instantiation of some functionalities such as Big Data analysis, development of context-aware applications, connection to the Internet of Things [15]. Existing architecture such as 5-level approach [11] generally focuses on design architecture and lacks consideration for modularity required for flexible predictive maintenance. On the other hand, FIWARE is a modular and open sourced platform, third parties or other software as required can be integrated via a plug in/out option [15], and hence is adopted in this work. In addition to acquiring modular feature, an architecture for predictive maintenance based on the concept of big data analytics and cloud computing is considered in this work. From the analysis and architecture of big data analytics systems in our previous work [7], the underlying functions and processes of the big data systems such as data collection, processing, modeling and analysis, and visualization, are realized for designing big data analytics required for predictive maintenance.

The proposed architecture generally consists of four main layers. The first layer is an *application layer* concerning applications, interfaces, dashboards, etc. The second layer is a *process layer* involves various processes. The third layer is a *middleware and data layer* concerning broker, adapters, data storage. The fourth layer contains a *resource layer* referring to factory resources e.g. production machines/equipment. Each layer has a general focus but is flexible enough to make up of different requirements i.e. processes, systems, tools, to meet different requirements. The architecture is controlled by identity access and management.

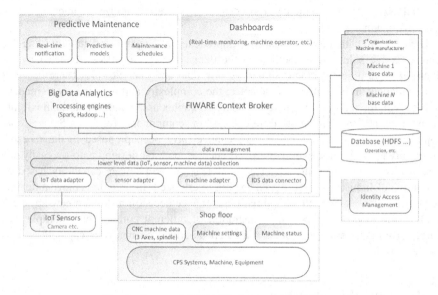

Fig. 1. Proposed FIWARE architecture platform.

At the resource layer i.e. the shop floor in Fig. 1, the framework gathers data from the shop floor, deployed sensors or devices deployed in the shop floor, which contains for example, operational machine data such as CNC operation data and spindle, CNC machine data, CNC assistant data, predefined CNC setting, machine statues, etc.

At the middleware and data layer, the FIWARE context broker acts as the core middleware in a publish and subscribe manner, accommodating the interaction of different processes, APIs, systems for the whole platform. Lower level data is collected using different data adapters, injecting into the Big data analytics processing engines for the process layer. Collected data is kept in storage like HDFS as required. In addition, machine measurement and basic machine data from the manufacturer is stored and managed in the industrial data space.

The process layer is implemented by the FIWARE framework, integrating different modules and functionalities required for predictive maintenance. The capability of big data analytics is essential for operating predictive maintenance in modern manufacturing described in Sect. 2. Thus, the core function of the proposed predictive maintenance platform is big data analytics, enabling big data analytics including batch and streaming data analytics processing incorporating with different data from sensor, Hadoop Distributed File System (HDFS), the platform database and other related manufacturing systems. The analytics can be available via the context broker's APIs for the functionalities of the application layer as a publish/subscribe manner.

For the application layer, the FIWARE context broker will collect data from different resources via various adapters or sensor enabled devices. This is used to fill the top-level Dashboards for monitoring purposes as well as inform predictive maintenance modules for maintenance scheduling purposes.

3.2 Predictive Maintenance Methods

As Industry 4.0 associates with IoT, big data and cloud computing, data driven approach is the cost-effective option compared with the model-based and experience-based approaches which are highly complex, difficult to build and maintain [6]. Hence, data driven approach is adopted in this work. A general data driven predictive maintenance approach includes data acquisition, data preprocessing, development of detection or prediction model and deployment and integration of the developed model [16]. In the case of Industry 4.0, multiple different machines/equipment involve in the production chain, hence further considerations such as multiple resources, machines, data fusion and processing, etc., are recognized.

In the case of RUL and tool wear detection aspects such as failure, degradation, various data such as manufacturing machine/equipment operational data collected via sensor are used to build models, capturing time sequence information [5, 10]. Methods such as sliding window, Hidden Markov Model (HMM) and Recurrent Neural Network (RNN) are widely used [10]. However, these approaches face challenges; computational complexity and storage with HMM, memory problems with RNN [17, 18]. Long Short-Term Memory Network (LSTM), a type of RNN, overcomes the memory problems by controlling information flow using gates (input, forget and output) [19]. Due to the nature of sequential sensor data, LSTM is suitable for data driven predictive models for machine condition and RUL. The approach for learning LSTM model in this work is presented in Fig. 2. The step can be iterative i.e. evaluate model to train model, etc., and adjusted to different needs i.e. parameter or network settings, autoencoder, etc., as required to the learning purpose.

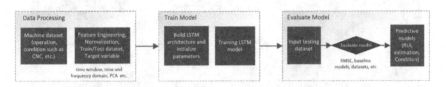

Fig. 2. Procedure of LSTM model

To support the aspect of predictive maintenance within the Big data analytics of the process layer, the predictive models in Fig. 1, combining data derived from the machine tool operator, manufacturer and sensors are used for developing the predictive models following the steps in Fig. 2, and are predicting the machine condition (e.g. worn) and remaining useful life (RUL) [5, 6, 10].

As in the case of real-time monitoring and notification in Fig. 1, the underlying machines, devices and factories are considered as the maintenance items. During operation, real-time state data collected from the underlying machine is processed by comparing the key state of each maintenance item including the threshold [5]. The state and threshold of the equipment item is stored in the maintenance repository in a database. Based on the notification of machine condition and RUL, maintenance schedule can be planned, and appropriate tasks can then be decided and performed for optimal operation.

4   FIWARE Predictive Maintenance for Application Case

A flexible manufacturing factory consists of a processing system, a logistics system, an information system, and an auxiliary system, collaborating multiple partners and customers. A concrete scene of the flexible factory is shown in Fig. 3. The processing system in the scene consists of 4 sets of equipment, which consists of an automatic stereoscopic warehouse, numbers of AGV trolleys, three robots, numbers of frames of carrier plates. Coordinate measuring machine (CMM) is responsible for the measurement. A cleaning machine and a drying machine are responsible for cleaning and drying the workpiece. Production data are typically generated by different machines equipment operation, condition, setting, etc., including CNC machine tool.

Fig. 3. Flexible manufacturing factory [5]

In the context of flexible manufacturing in this case, data are collected from different machines and tools via sensor as well as other information systems like ERP, MES, etc. Also, the manufacturing industries work beyond their boundary i.e. collaborative partners, suppliers, etc., and the nature of dynamic data can be extremely frequent and highly voluminous in the context of modern factory [1, 2, 5]. Thus, it is essential to use a consistent but extensible model to allow for a flexible predictive maintenance in manufacturing. FIWARE offers a data model based on an entity-attribute model, the entities are used to represent and model real world objects including virtual entities, the attributes that describe different aspects of the entity as well as supporting open standards and extensibility [15]. In this aspect, FIWARE model meets the requirements of flexible predictive maintenance platform, thus it is adopted for the application case as presented in Fig. 4.

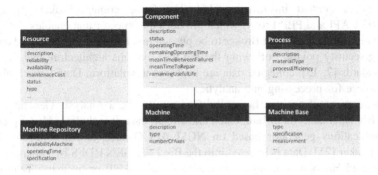

Fig. 4. Sample machine data model

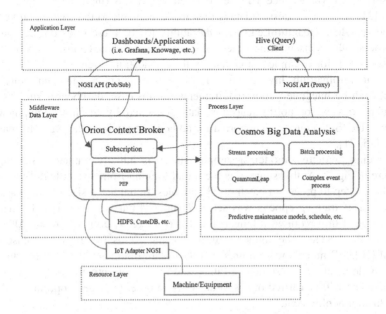

Fig. 5. Propose FIWARE predictive maintenance Case

The proposed architecture in Fig. 1 is instantiated for the application case in Fig. 3 using key components enabling Big Data Analytics within FIWARE framework in Fig. 5 with the LSTM predictive models in Sect. 3.2 and data model in Fig. 4.

At the **resource layer**, different machines/devices are used for production, connected via associated adapters enabling the interaction with the context broker and related data processes and storage using the proposed data model. For seamlessly connecting, managing and gathering data of IoT devices in this case, FIWARE generic enablers such as IoT Agent for JSON, and OPC-UA, as well as Ultralight 2.0 protocol and NGSI for complex real-time processing are configured as required.

For the middleware and data layer, Orion Context Broker as the middleware represents a Publish/Subscribe Context Broker Generic Enabler hosted within the predictive maintenance platform. It provides services including the registration of provider systems, updates and notifications based on changes in context information, and query of context information [15]. The Orion context broker utilizes the NGSI REST API and PEP Proxy, which provides a connector that enables the context data coming from the Context Broker to be pushed into HDFS storage as the data layer enforcing security policy. Following the big data systems architecture and FIWARE open standards [7, 15], collected data are kept into the platform Data Lake enabling a central source for processing and analytics.

In the context of **process layer**, the Cosmos Big Data Analysis Generic Enabler enables Big Data analysis of both batch and stream data. It includes a Hadoop engine, an authentications generator based on NGSI API Oauth2, and a connector to the Context Broker [21]. Data is injected into the Big Data GE's HDFS by either accessing the integrated Hadoop command line interface via a shell, or by using Telefonica's SSH File Transfer Protocol (SFTP) server for direct data injection into HDFS [21, 22]. The results from MapReduce will be accessed via HDFS (input and output folders created) [21, 22]. The processed data is then made available to the context broker. For real-time analytics, QuantumLeap with the ability to configure rules on the complex event process allows instant time-series data pushed by machine equipment, which then can be available, for example via Gafana at the application layer.

For **the application layer**, different dashboards, applications and other user interfaces can be integrated upon requirements. In this case, dashboards such as Grafana offers to view or notify real-time data generated by machine equipment. In addition, Hive (SQL) query is supported for ad hoc query within the big data analytics module [15, 21].

Regarding predictive model, a sample dataset is initially trained, following the procedure in Fig. 2. At this stage, it is the initial training from a sample dataset 12000 with 30 time step to process a batch of 28 variables. Initial batch size of 750 was used. The number of training epochs was set at 71 epochs but was increased for datasets where the algorithm required a longer time to converge. A dropout rate of 20% were used after the LSTM. The model is trained using Keras library with TensorFlow backend [20]. All models were trained via the Adam optimizer. The sample data and initial sample result are presented in Fig. 6 and Fig. 7 respectively. Full analysis and model learning will be carried out as future work in order to achieve optimized models for production deployment.

In addition to utilizing LSTM predictive models, actual operating time can be calculated, and the remaining operating time until maintenance is subsequently determined using the proposed data model in Fig. 4 [5, 23]. Furthermore, the remaining operating life of the machine equipment can be calculated by the extended Taylor's equation, obtaining the values of the parameters including the speed, the feed rate, and the properties of the machine tool material and the workpiece as well as KPIs [23].

The information about the machine equipment stored in the machine repository proposed in the data model is available via the dashboard, which is also accessible to the digital twins for available machine equipment. This includes, the design of each machine and its configuration capability such as the workpiece, etc., and the information related to the available machines and their parameters. This enables the maintenance operators who create the process plan, obtaining the information about the availability of the resources for creating viable process plans via the dashboard.

To support transparent collaboration in the proposed platform, machine base data is accessed via the FIWARE's IDS connector, facilitating the transparency of policy, data flow, usage and access across the interactions between each component with the context broker on the platform. To gain greater scalability of the proposed architecture, FIWARE offered container virtualization using container images is adopted for deployment [24].

Feature	Data Type
Machine process	int
Machine sequence number	int
Machine	int
Machine condition	int
Feed rate	float
Camp pressure	float
Axis (X, Y, Z)	float

(a)

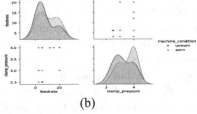

(b)

Fig. 6. (a) Sample machine dataset (b) Sample machine operational data

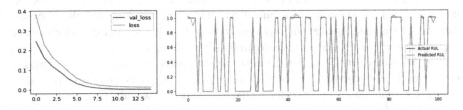

Fig. 7. Initial result from sample dataset

5 Discussion

Modern manufacturing such as the application case in Fig. 3 is complex and involves modern plant-run machines deployed smart sensors (sensor networks), network of collaborative partners and processes, and robots running on the shop floor. Flexibility is critical for the whole production chain, in the sense that the existing systems e.g. machines can easily be integrated with predictive maintenance, and other different systems or processes without significant effort. In other words, interoperability i.e. the ease integration of the existing machines, robots, systems, etc. and predictive maintenance platform is highly important. Existing approach [11] offers 5-level architecture for Industry 4.0 manufacturing systems, however it lacks the consideration for modularity, collaboration, middleware component or big data analytics implementation.

The proposed solution however aims to provide flexible and modular architecture using FIWARE framework in Fig. 5. The flexibility is achieved by facilitating the ease integration of different components required for predictive maintenance. The proposed 4-layer approach, like 5-level approach [11] supports better understanding of different components/processes at different levels as well as the overall architecture. Our adoption of FIWARE framework also provides the modularity which facilitates the ease integration i.e. interoperability of different components as pluggable components. In this sense, the case's current different machines, robots, systems and other information systems like MES, ERP, Logistics, CRM, etc., can be easily integrated with the designed predictive maintenance solution, enabling effective maintenance analytics with minimal effort.

Besides, middleware technology which is not considered in existing 5-level architecture [11], is the basis for any IoT system to manage effective communications/interactions i.e. machine to machine, machine to system, etc. within a context. The adopted FIWARE context broker along with Big Data Analysis module facilitates the support for the interaction and integration of existing as well as future different IoT devices within the production plant as well as other collaborative context for information analytics.

In the context of collaboration in the described case, various collaborative processes exist in the form of network of machines and systems as well as network of collaborations i.e. machine manufacturers, suppliers, insurers, customers, etc. In other words, data interaction occurs at different levels i.e. components, machines, systems. Also, collaborative data are moved/accessed; machine base data from manufacturer, product design data from partner as well as machine status/diagnosis required to the insurer for purposes e.g. claim analysis. The application of IDS connector along with the proposed data model facilitates greater interoperability as well as greater transparency of data access due to the policy and usage controls of the IDS connector in a collaborative context. Ultimately, it will facilitate virtual factory production mode which requires a higher level of integration of data from customers, suppliers and partners across enterprises, enabling the optimization of the information flow and delivery process for smart plant information systems.

In the case of maintenance in the presented case, effective maintenance is essential to decreasing the costs associated with downtime and faulty products. The proposed solution currently focuses on predictive maintenance in the manner that maintenance activity can be carried out before a potential failure or a degradation of a machine/equipment is detected. On the other hand, without the process of optimal maintenance schedule plan for the existing complex machines/equipment within the production chain, it is not easy to manage effective maintenance. In this regard, optimal maintenance schedule plan considering complex systems, cost, etc., in the context of Industry 4.0, will be hugely significant for future work.

6 Conclusion

In this paper, we proposed flexible and modular Predictive Maintenance using FIWARE to overcome some challenges of predictive maintenance in modern collaborative manufacturing. Predictive maintenance in industry collaborations in the complex and dynamic manufacturing environment requires a concrete, extensible architecture and platform. Unlike the 5-level approach, the proposed predictive maintenance platform offers flexible and modular system with advanced capabilities to handle the requirements of Industry 4.0 and advanced analytics e.g. LSTM models (machine condition, RUL). The effectiveness of the proposed solution is demonstrated within a flexible manufacturing case. Using predictive maintenance analytics, the maintenance task can be performed in an efficient manner to avoid unnecessary downtime, to keep low cost and to provide better management of the condition and process of expensive manufacturing equipment and optimization of the whole production chain. Regarding future work, we plan to do the implementation and evaluation of the design platform including predictive models, with the described application case and further use cases across industries as well as the development of optimal predictive maintenance schedule plan considering complex systems of Industry 4.0.

Acknowledgements. This research is partially funded by the State Key Research and Development Program of China (2017YFE0118700) and it is part of the FIRST project which has received funding from the European Union's Horizon 2020 research and innovation programme under the Marie Skłodowska-Curie grant agreement No 734599.

References

1. Thoben, K.D., Wiesner, S., Wuest, T.: "Industrie 4.0" and smart manufacturing-a review of research issues and application examples. Int. J. Autom. Technol. 11(1), 4–16 (2017)
2. Koren, Y., Gu, X., Guo, W.: Reconfigurable manufacturing systems: principles, design, and future trends. Front. Mech. Eng. 13(2), 121–136 (2018). https://doi.org/10.1007/s11465-018-0483-0
3. Mobley, R.K.: An Introduction to Predictive Maintenance. Butterworth-Heinemann, Oxford (2002)
4. Wang, L.: Machine availability monitoring and machining process planning towards cloud manufacturing. CIRP J. Manuf. Sci. Technol. 6(4), 263–273 (2013)
5. Sang, G.M., Xu, L., de Vrieze, P., Bai, Y., Pan, F.: Predictive maintenance in Industry 4.0. In: ICIST 2020: 10th International Conference on Information Systems and Technologies, 4–5 June 2020
6. Tobon-Mejiaab, D.A., Medjahera, K., Zerhouni, N.: CNC machine tool's wear diagnostic and prognostic by using dynamic Bayesian networks. Mech. Syst. Sig. Process. 28, 167–182 (2012)

7. Sang, G.M., Xu, L., de Vrieze, P.: Simplifying big data analytics systems with a reference architecture. In: Camarinha-Matos, L.M., Afsarmanesh, H., Fornasiero, R. (eds.) PRO-VE 2017. IAICT, vol. 506, pp. 242–249. Springer, Cham (2017). https://doi.org/10.1007/978-3-319-65151-4_23

8. Debevec, M., Simic, M., Herakovic, N.: Virtual factory as an advanced approach for production process optimization. Int. J. Simul. Modell. **13**(1), 66–78 (2014)

9. Xu, L., de Vrieze, P., Yu, H., Phalp, K., Bai, Y.: Interoperability of virtual factory: an overview of concepts and research challenges. Int. J. Mech. Manuf. Syst. (2020)

10. Si, X.S., Wang, W., Hu, C.H., Zhou, D.H.: Remaining useful life estimation–a review on the statistical data driven approaches. Eur. J. Oper. Res. **213**(1), 1–14 (2011)

11. Lee, J., Baheri, B., Kao, H.: A cyber-physical systems architecture for Industry 4.0-based manufacturing systems. Manuf. Lett. **3**, 18–23 (2015)

12. Wang, J., Zhang, L., Duan, L., Gao, R.X.: A new paradigm of cloud-based predictive maintenance for intelligent manufacturing. J. Intell. Manuf. **28**(5), 1125–1137 (2017). https://doi.org/10.1007/s10845-015-1066-0

13. Hribernik, K., von Stietencron, M., Bousdekis, A., Bredehorst, B., Mentzas, G., Thoben, K. D.: Towards a unified predictive maintenance system-a use case in production logistics in aeronautics. Procedia Manuf. **16**, 131–138 (2018)

14. Guillén, A.J., Crespo, A., Gómez, J.F., Sanz, M.D.: A framework for effective management of condition based maintenance programs in the context of industrial development of E-Maintenance strategies. Comput. Ind. **82**(2016), 170–185 (2016)

15. FIWARE Catalogue (2020). https://www.fiware.org/developers/catalogue/. Accessed 20 Jan 2020

16. Mathworks (2020). https://www.mathworks.com/help/predmaint/gs/designing-algorithms-for-condition-monitoring-and-predictive-maintenance.html. Accessed 20 Feb 2020

17. Baruah, P., Chinnam, R.B.: HMMs for diagnostics and prognostics in machining processes. Int. J. Prod. Res. **43**(6), 1275–1293 (2005)

18. Bengio, Y., Simard, P., Frasconi, P.: Learning long-term dependencies with gradient descent is difficult. IEEE Trans. Neural Netw. **5**(2), 157–166 (1994)

19. Hochreiter, S., Schmidhuber, J.: Long short-term memory. Neural Comput. **9**(8), 1735–1780 (1997)

20. Goodfellow, I., Bengio, Y., Courville, A.: Deep Learning. MIT Press, Cambridge (2016)

21. FIWARE Big Data Analysis (2020). https://fiware-tutorials.readthedocs.io/en/latest/big-data-analysis/index.html. Accessed 20 Feb 2020

22. Apache Hadoop (2020). http://hadoop.apache.org/. Accessed 20 Feb 2020

23. Teti, R., Jemielniak, K., O'Donnell, G., Dornfeld, D.: Advanced monitoring of machining operations. CIRP Ann. **59**(2), 717–739 (2010)

24. FIWARE Docker Container Service (2020). https://fiware-docker-container-service.readthedocs.io/en/latest/index.html. Accessed 20 Feb 2020

An Architecture for Predictive Maintenance of Railway Points Based on Big Data Analytics

Giulio Salierno[1]([✉])(iD), Sabatino Morvillo[2], Letizia Leonardi[1](iD), and Giacomo Cabri[1](iD)

[1] Università di Modena e Reggio Emilia, Modena, Italy
{giulio.salierno,letizia.leonardi,giacomo.cabri}@unimore.it
[2] Alstom Ferroviaria S.p.A, Savigliano, Italy
sabatino.morvillo@alstomgroup.com

Abstract. Massive amounts of data produced by railway systems are a valuable resource to enable Big Data analytics. Despite its richness, several challenges arise when dealing with the deployment of a big data architecture into a railway system. In this paper, we propose a four-layers big data architecture with the goal of establishing a data management policy to manage massive amounts of data produced by railway switch points and perform analytical tasks efficiently. An implementation of the architecture is given along with the realization of a Long Short-Term Memory prediction model for detecting failures on the Italian Railway Line of Milano - Monza - Chiasso.

Keywords: Railway data · Predictive maintenance · Big data architecture

1 Introduction

In recent years, Big Data analytics has gained relevant interest from both industries and academia thanks to its possibilities to open up new shapes of data analysis as well as its essential role in the decision-making processes of enterprises. Different studies [8], highlight the importance of big data, among other sectors, for the railway industries. The insight offered by big data analytics covers different areas of the railway industry, including and not limited to *maintenance*, *safety*, *operation*, and *customer satisfaction*. In fact, according to the growing demand for railway transportation, the analysis of the huge amount of data produced by the railway world has a positive impact not only in the services offered to the customers but also for the railway providers. Knowledge extracted from raw data enables railway operators to optimize the maintenance costs and enforce the safety and reliability of the railway infrastructure by the adoption of

This work was partially supported by the EU H2020 program under Grant No. 734599 - FIRST project.

S. Dupuy-Chessa and H. A. Proper (Eds.): CAiSE 2020 Workshops, LNBIP 382, pp. 29–40, 2020.
https://doi.org/10.1007/978-3-030-49165-9_3

new analytical tools based on descriptive and predictive analysis. Maintenance of railway lines encompasses different elements placed along the railway track, including but not limited to signals and points. Our interest is mainly on predictive maintenance tasks that aim to build a variety of models with the scope of monitoring the health status of the points composing the line. Typical predicting metrics of Remaining Useful Life (RUL) and Time To Failure (TTF) enable predictive maintenance by estimating healthy status of objects and replacing them before failures occur. Despite unquestionable value of big data for the railway companies, according to [3] big data analytics is not fully adopted by them, yet due to different aspects mainly related with the lack of understanding on how big data can be deployed into railway transportation systems and the lack of efficient collection and analysis of massive amount of data. The goal of our work is to design a big data architecture for enabling analytical tasks typical required by the railway industry as well as enabling an effective data management policy to allows end-users to manage huge amounts of data coming from railway lines efficiently. As already mentioned, we considered predictive maintenance as the main task of our architecture; hence to show the effectiveness of the proposed architecture, we use real data collected from points placed over the Italian railway line (Milano - Monza - Chiasso). The complexity of the considered system poses different challenges for enabling efficient management of the huge amount of data. The first challenge concerns the collection of the data given the heterogeneity of the data sources. Multiple railway points produce distinct log files, which must be collected and processed efficiently. The second challenge is to deal with the data itself. Data collected from the system must be stored as raw data without any modification to preserve the original data in case of necessity (e.g., in case of failures, further analyses require to analyze data at a higher level of granularity). At the same time, collected data must be processed and transformed to be useful for analysis thus, data must be pre-processed and aggregated before fitting models for analytics. Finally, the data analysis performed by the end-users requires analytical models to perform predictive or descriptive analysis; thus, the architecture should enable model creation as well as graphical visualization of results.

The paper is organized as follows. Section 2 describes similar works that discuss the design of Big Data architectures for railways systems. Section 3 describes the kinds of data produced by a railway system. Sections 4 and 5 describe, respectively, the architectural design and its implementation. The Sect. 6 presents a real case scenario in which failure prediction is performed on real data. Section 7 draws some conclusions.

2   Related Work

To the best of our knowledge, few solutions take into consideration challenges arisen when deploying a big data architecture for railway systems. Most works focus on theoretical frameworks where simulations produce results without experimenting with real data. Moreover, researchers mainly focus on Machine

Learning algorithms as well as analytical models, giving less importance to the fundamental tasks related to data management, ingestion processing, and storage. Close to our work in [9], authors propose a cloud-based big data architecture for real-time analysis of data produced by on-board equipment of high-speed trains. However, the proposed architecture presents scalability issues since it is not possible to deploy large-scale computing clusters in high-speed trains; neither is it possible to deploy a fully cloud-based architecture due to bandwidth limitation of trains which make infeasible transferring huge amount of data to the cloud to perform real-time analysis. On the contrary, the scope of our work is to define a scalable Big Data architecture for enabling analytical tasks using railway data. For this reason and due to space limit, we have reported only work related to the railway scenario.

3   Data Produced by a Railway Interlocking System

In our work, we take into consideration the data log files produced by a railway interlocking system. A railway interlocking is a complex safety-critical system that ensures the establishment of routes for trains through a railway yard [1]. The computer-based interlocking system guarantees that no critical-safety condition (i.e., a train circulate in a track occupied by another train) will arise during the train circulation. Among other actions issued by the interlocking, before the route is composed, it checks the state of each point along the line. The interlocking system produces log files that store information about the command issued to the point as well as data about its behavior. Commands are issued by the interlocking through smart boards, which in turn control the physical point on the line and collect data about their status. Once data are collected, they are written into the data storage of the interlocking system as log files. These log files can be both structured and semi-structured data and contain diverse information about the behavior of the points upon the requests sent by the interlocking system. Requests may vary according to the logic that must be executed to set up a route (e.g., a switch point is moved from the normal to the reverse position or vice versa) and this implies that the information contained in log files may vary. A complete railway line is controlled by multiple interlocking systems, which in turn produce different log files according to the points they control. The analytical task which motivates the design of our architecture is the prediction of failures. A failure may occur when a mechanical part of points has a break. This kind of failure propagates negatively on the entire railway traffic; therefore, its prediction is desirable. Moreover, instead of doing maintenance when a failure occurs, it is also useful in particular, to estimate the RUL of point in order to enable predictive maintenance by estimating if a points will fail or not in a certain time-frame. Predicting failures of railway points requires to take into consideration the log files produced by the interlocking whenever a command is issued to a point. These log files are heterogeneous in type and contain different information resumed as:

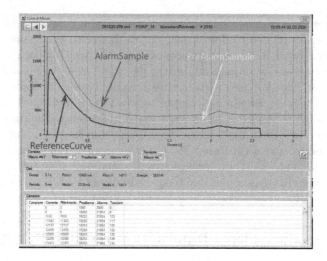

Fig. 1. Graphical visualization of data sample collected from a switch point

1. Timestamps respectively indicating the time recorded the logging server upon submitting the command, and the timestamp recorded by the smartboard when an action is performed.
2. Information about the smartboard that controls the point (channel number, name of the smartboard, sampling frequency).
3. Information about the operation issued by the interlocking (type of movement, total number of movements, number of current movement in a single day).
4. A set of raw data representing values of Voltage and Power supplied to the point to operate.

Data 3 and 4 are considered to train and evaluate the proposed model to estimate the health status of the points, thus to estimate its RUL (see Sect. 5). As an example, we report a sample collected from a railway switch point (Fig. 1). These samples contain three types of information:

1. **ReferenceCurve**: is a sample curve representing the behavior of the point upon the command issued by the interlocking. This curve is used to derive the following ones;
2. **PreAlarmSample**: is a pre-threshold curve, computed by adding to the ReferenceCurve an intermediate threshold value;
3. **AlarmSample**: is the alarm curve computed as the previous one by adding an alarm threshold value.

4   System Architecture

The Big Data architecture presented in this section covers all the fundamental stages of a big data pipeline [4] of:

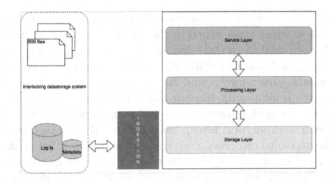

Fig. 2. Architecture for railway big data management

1. Data acquisition by implementing ingestion tasks for collecting data from external sources.
2. Information extraction and retrieval by processing ingested data and storing them in a raw format.
3. Data integration, aggregation, and representation by data table view as well as data aggregation functionalities to produce new data for analytics.
4. Modeling and analysis by providing a set of functionalities to build models to perform predictive analytics.
5. Interpretation of results by graphical visualization of data.

The architecture presented in Fig. 2 includes the following layers:

Storage layer is the layer responsible for implementing the data storage. It contains the storage platform to provide a distributed and fault-tolerant filesystem. In particular, this layer, should store data in their raw form. Therefore datasets for analytic models will be originated from the upper layers.

Processing layer provides all tasks for data manipulation/transformation useful for the analytical layer. In particular, this layer presents a structured view of the data of the Storage layer, allowing the creation of datasets by transforming raw data coming from the Storage layer. The structured view of data is implemented through table views of the raw data. The transformation of original data is performed through aggregation functions provided by this layer.

Service layer contains all components to provide analytics as a service to the end-users. This layer interacts with the processing layer in order to access data stored on the platform, manipulate and transform data to fit analytical models. In addition, it provides: 1) Data visualization functionalities for graphical displaying data 2) Models creation to perform analytical tasks.

Ingestion layer This layer implements all the tasks for the ingestion of data from external sources. It is based on ingestion tools, which enable the definition of dataflows. A dataflow consists of a variable number of processes that transform data by the creation of flow files that are moved from one processor to another through process relations. A relation is a connection between two processors to define data flow policies among data flow processes.

Our architecture is an implementation of the concept of a datalake [2]. To avoid situations in which data stored in the platform become not usable due to multiple challenges related to their complexity, size, variety, and lack of metadata, we adopt a mechanism of URI[1] abstraction to simplify data access, thus establishing a data governance policy. As an example, at the storage layer, the URI of a resource is simply its absolute path. In order, to avoid the definition of multiples URIs for each resource (since they can be used by multiple components at different architectural layer), we define a URI abstraction mechanism to simplify the access to resources since they are stored in a distributed manner (where keeping track of the physical location of a resources could be tricky). Therefore the *RealURI* refers to a resource stored on the distributed filesystem abstracting its physical location. A *RealURI* is bound to a single *VirtualURI*, which is in charge of abstracting the details of paths adopted by a particular implementation of a distributed filesystems. A *PresentationURI* is an optional URI created whenever a component of the Processing layer or Service layer uses a resource stored on the filesystem. As an example, the URI abstractions defined for a single resource are reported in Table 1. Each resource is identified by 1) a smartboard id, 2) a channel number that controls a specific point, 3) a point number which identifies the object on the line. These metadata are extracted from the data described in Sect. 3. through the tasks provided by the Ingestion layer described in the next section. In addition, the *VirtualURI* refers to the resource at a platform level, while the *PresentationURI* represents a HIVE table view of the data created by the processing layer (see Sect. 5). We stress the fact that while resources can be assigned to an unbounded number of *PresentationURI*, depending on the type of components that consume the data, the *VirtualURI* is mandatory and it refers to a single *RealURI*.

Table 1. URI abstractions for storage resources

URI type	URI	View level
RealURI	`hdfs://data_path/smart_board_number/channel/point_number`	Filesystem
VirtualURI	`adc://data_path/smart_board_number/channel/point_number`	Platform
PresentationURI	`adc:hive://data_path/smart_board_number/channel/point_number`	Analytics

5 Architecture Implementation

The architecture has been implemented mainly using components of the Hadoop[2] stack. Hadoop is a framework that allows for the distributed processing of large data sets across clusters of computers using simple commodity-hardware. Hadoop provides different components to implement a complete big data architecture. In particular, for this work, we considered:

---

[1] An Uniform Resource Identifier (URI) is a sequence of characters that uniquely identify resources on a system.
[2] http://hadoop.apache.org/.

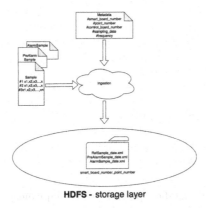

HDFS - storage layer

Fig. 3. Ingestion process to store data and related metadata

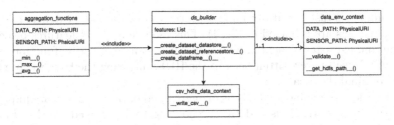

Fig. 4. Class diagram of the dataset builder module

Storage layer, which has been implemented using the Hadoop Filesystem named HDFS. HDFS is a fault-tolerant distributed filesystem that runs on cluster providing fault-tolerance and high availability of the data. HDFS stores raw data as ingested by the Ingestion layer, as represented in Fig. 3. In particular, the Ingestion layer performs extraction of data and metadata and aggregate data into a specific folder stored on HDFS representing data for a particular point. Data representing point behavior (see Sect. 3) are stored in their original format as XML files. Therefore these data must be processed and transformed to create new datasets. This task is performed by the processing layer.

Processing layer Before data can be employed into analysis must be transformed to fulfill the requirements of analytical models. The processing layer implements all the tasks required to build datasets from raw data. This layer has been implemented through the specification of two components. The first component has the scope of processing raw XML files by extracting relevant features and aggregating them into CSV files, thus producing new datasets. Results are written back to the HDFS in the folder of the original data provenance. This mechanism allows enriching the data available, producing aggregation of raw data as well as providing features extraction functionalities to extract/aggregate features to be used by analytical models.

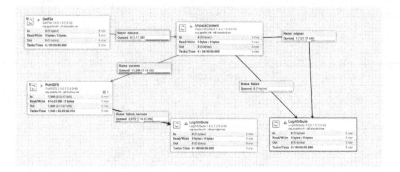

Fig. 5. Example of a NiFi dataflow pipeline which implement an ingestion task from a local filesystem

To fulfill this task, a dataset builder processes raw data and extracts relevant features (classes are reported in Fig. 4). This module extracts features provided as input and aggregates them into CSV files using an aggregation function (min, max, avg). Results are written back to the HDFS utilizing the HDFS context to get the original data path.

In addition, to enable an analysis of aggregated data, these files are imported into HIVE tables. HIVE is a data warehousing tool provided by the Hadoop stack, which includes a SQL-like language (HIVEQL) to query data. To import data into HIVE tables, we define a general schema to match the structure of data points. The table schema for representing data points is read from the aggregated CSV created by the dataset builder. A general table schema representing data for a generic point is structured as:

```
smart_board_number_point_number(RecordSampleTime DATE,
MovTime FLOAT, current_mA FLOAT, voltage_V FLOAT)
```

The designed HIVE tables store aggregated data containing the extracted features obtained from raw data. Results of aggregation extract four features respectively representing: 1) a timestamp in which sample was collected, 2) the estimated time to complete the operation, 3) the average current expressed in mA issued by the point 4) the average voltage V. Features 2, 3 and 4 are obtained by the aggregation of single measurements contained in the original data.

Service layer acts as a presentation layer. It implements all the tasks needed to build models for analytics as well as graphical visualize data. These tasks are fulfilled by Jupyter notebooks. Notebooks are designed to support the workflow of scientific computing, from interactive exploration to publishing a detailed record of computation. The code in a notebook is organized into cells, chunks which can be individually modified and run. The output from each cell appears directly below it and is stored as part of the document [5]. In addition, a variety of languages supported by notebooks allows integrating different open-source tools for data analysis like Numpy, Pandas, and Matplot [7]. These tools allow to parse data in a structured format and to perform data manipulation and visualization by built-in libraries. In addition, the data structure adopted by Pandas, named, DataFrame, is widely adopted as input format by a variety of analytical models offered via machine learning libraries like scikit-learn and SciPy.

Ingestion layer has been realized through Apache NiFi, a dataflow system based on the concepts of flow-based programming. Dataflows specify a path that describes how data are extracted from the external sources and stored on the platform. An example of DataFlow, which combines data coming from an external filesystem, is provided in Fig. 5. The flow files created by the dataflow are then written to the HDFS. In the reported example, the files read from a local filesystem are unpacked and then written into a specific folder on the HDFS. This folder is created by extracting meaningful information necessary to identify the smartboard where the data comes from as well as the point which produced that data.

The proposed architecture has been employed for the collection and processing of data of the railway line Milano-Monza-Chiasso. This line is composed of 72 points forming the railway track, which are managed by multiple smart boards that collect data. In particular, data are collected from 7 points which produces roughly 32 GB/month. Data produced by the system contains information about points status and type of commands issued by the interlocking to move points. The definition of a data management policy allows to collects, govern, and controls raw data as well as enabling data analysis for end-users. The proposed platform has been deployed in a test environment using a containerization technology Fig. 6.

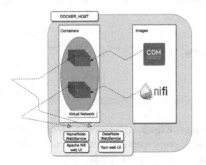

Fig. 6. Architecture deployment using containers.

We adopted two separate containers, which respectively implement the data storage & processing layers plus the ingestion layer in a separate environment. These containers communicate over a virtual network, which allows exchanging data in an isolated environment exposing web services to access the platforms and perform tasks. This deployment enables scalability of the architecture by moving containers on a cluster. Cloudera pre-built image has been adopted as a container implementing the Hadoop stack, while a separate container based on

Apache NiFi has been proposed to perform the ingestion tasks. A docker image containing the proposed platform is made available for further testing[3].

6   Example of Failure Detection Using LSTM

As an example to show the effectiveness of the proposed architecture, we report the creation of a Long Short- Term Memory (LSTM) model for failure detection of a specific railway point along the railway line Milano-Monza-Chiasso. LSTM models are a special kind of Recurrent Neural Networks (RNN) widely employed by both Academia and Industries for failure prediction [6]. A key aspect of RNN is their ability to store information or cell state for use later to make new predictions. Therefore these aspects make them particularly suitable for analysis of temporal data like analysis of sensor readings for detecting anomalies. For the considered scenario, we use sensor reading collected from a specific switch point positioned along the line. Data originated from the point includes measurements of power supplied to the object, voltage, and time of movement (to move from a normal to a reversal position or vice-versa) of types described in Sect. 3 and reported in Fig. 2. Once data are ingested, we use components composing the Processing Layer to produce useful datasets for anomalies detection using the techniques described in the previous sections. Results of the aggregation process produce a dataset consisting of 2443 samples, which are used as input for training the model. The evaluation part is performed using reference data, which represents threshold values above which failures occur (89 samples). Examples of features used for training the model are reported in Fig. 7, 8, 9.

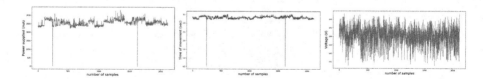

Fig. 7. Extracted feature used as model input, representing power supplied to a point   **Fig. 8.** Extracted feature representing time of movement in seconds   **Fig. 9.** Extracted feature representing emitted voltage

The autoencoder model used to make predictions learns a compressed representation of the input data and then learns to reconstruct them again. The idea is training the model on data not containing anomalies; therefore, the model will likely to be able to reconstruct healthy samples. We expect that until the model predicts healthy samples, its reconstruction error (representing the distance between the input and the reconstructed sample) is low. Whenever the model processes data outside the norm as the ones represented by the reference

---

[3] docker pull julio92sg/data:cloudera-hadoop-nifi.

data, which consist of threshold values, we expect an increase in the reconstruction error as the model was not trained to reconstruct these kinds of data. Therefore, we use the reconstruction error as an indicator for anomaly detection. Figure 10 reports anomalies detected by trying to predict reference values. In particular, we will see an increase of the reconstruction error on those values which are greater than a threshold of 0.25. This threshold was obtained by computing the error loss on the training set. Therefore, we identified this value suitable for the point considered as a case study, but it varies according to the particular behavior of the object. For example, considering two objects having the same characteristics (e.g., switch points) placed in different railway network topologies, may have different behaviors; therefore, they must be analyzed using different prediction models.

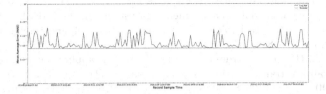

Fig. 10. Anomalies detection on a railway switch point of railway line Milano-Monza-Chiasso.

7   Conclusion

This paper proposes a novel architecture for big data management and analysis of railway data. Despite big data attract railways industries, many challenges have to be faced to enable effective big data analysis of railway data. This work proposes a four-layer architecture for enabling data analytics of railway points. Each layer is loosely coupled with others; therefore, it enables the integration of diverse data processing components intra-layers and inter-layers. To show the effectiveness of the proposed architecture, we reported the analysis of a railway switch points using predictive models for detecting failures. Nevertheless, instead of being task-oriented, the proposed architecture integrates different data processing tools to perform diverse analytical tasks as real-time data analysis. A data governance policy has been defined to deal with the variety and the complexity of railway data making them easily manageable at different granularity levels. A containerized deployment has been proposed to scale the architecture on a cluster, increasing up its scalability, thus enabling parallel data processing. Our architecture can also be extended according to the nature of the task to perform. In fact, it allows practitioners to extend architectural components to fulfil different tasks not limited to failure prediction. Moreover, in this work, we did not consider any real-time scenario in which data must be analyzed using streaming techniques, but the architecture flexibility also allows to deal with such cases. As future work, the analytical layer will be extended, proposing a comparison of different classes of predictive algorithms to measure their accuracy in diverse predictive maintenance tasks of a railway system. Moreover, we aim to extend the scope of the architecture by monitoring other kinds of infrastructures, including but not limited to power grids and highways intelligent systems.

References

1. Banci, M., Fantechi, A.: Geographical versus functional modelling bystatecharts of interlocking systems. Electron. Notes Theor. Comput. Sci. **133**, 3–19 (2005). https://doi.org/10.1016/j.entcs.2004.08.055. Proceedings of the Ninth International Workshop on Formal Methods for Industrial Critical Systems (FMICS 2004)
2. Fang, H.: Managing data lakes in big data era: what's a data lake and why has it became popular in data management ecosystem. In: 2015 IEEE International Conference on Cyber Technology in Automation, Control, and Intelligent Systems (CYBER), pp. 820–824, June 2015. https://doi.org/10.1109/CYBER.2015.7288049
3. Ghofrani, F., He, Q., Goverde, R.M., Liu, X.: Recent applications of big data analytics in railway transportation systems: a survey. Transp. Res. Part C: Emerg. Technol. **90**, 226–246 (2018). https://doi.org/10.1016/j.trc.2018.03.010
4. Jagadish, H.V., et al.: Big data and its technical challenges. Commun. ACM **57**(7), 86–94 (2014). https://doi.org/10.1145/2611567
5. Kluyver, T., et al.: Jupyter notebooks ? A publishing format for reproducible computational workflows. In: Loizides, F., Scmidt, B. (eds.) Positioning and Power in Academic Publishing: Players, Agents and Agendas, pp. 87–90. IOS Press (2016). https://eprints.soton.ac.uk/403913/
6. Meyes, R., Donauer, J., Schmeing, A., Meisen, T.: A recurrent neural network architecture for failure prediction in deep drawing sensory time series data. Procedia Manuf. **34**, 789–797 (2019). https://doi.org/10.1016/j.promfg.2019.06.205. 47th SME North American Manufacturing Research Conference, NAMRC 47, Pennsylvania, USA
7. Nelli, F.: Python Data Analytics: With Pandas, NumPy, and Matplotlib, 2nd edn. Apress, USA (2018)
8. Thaduri, A., Galar, D., Kumar, U.: Railway assets: a potential domain for bigdata analytics. Procedia Comput. Sci. **53**, 457–467 (2015). https://doi.org/10.1016/j.procs.2015.07.323. iNNS Conference on BigData 2015 Program San Francisco, CA, USA 8-10 August 2015
9. Xu, Q., et al.: A platform for fault diagnosis of high-speed train based on big data - project supported by the national natural science foundation, china (61490704, 61440015) and the national high-tech. r&d program, China (no. 2015aa043802). IFAC-Papers OnLine **51**(18), 309–314 (2018). https://doi.org/10.1016/j.ifacol.2018.09.318. 10th IFAC Symposium on Advanced Control of Chemical Processes ADCHEM 2018

Integration Framework of MES Toward Data Security Interoperation

Shuangyu Wei[1], Yuewei Bai[1(✉)], Lai Xu[2], Hua Mu[3], Kai Liu[1], and Xiaogang Wang[1]

[1] Shanghai Polytechnic University, Pudong 201209, Shanghai, China
ywbai@sspu.edu.cn
[2] Bournemouth University, Bournemouth BH12 5BB, UK
[3] KM Information Technology Co., Ltd., Wuhan 430000, Hubei, China

Abstract. The core problem of the application of MES (Manufacturing Execution System) in intelligent manufacturing systems is integration, which solves the problem of the data interoperation between the distributed manufacturing systems. The previous researches on MES integration rarely considered the problem of system data security access. A three-level data security access mechanism based on the independence of the system administrators, security administrators, and security auditors is proposed which integrated into the MES integration framework to guarantee the business and engineering data security access for the related distributed clients. The principle is using the domain to make the logical isolation for different clients and data sources and applying the pre-defined data sharing rules for safe access. In the proposed MES integration framework model, the data interoperation between MES and the engineering software systems is discussed which includes ERP (Enterprise Resource Management), CAPP (Computer Aided Process Planning), DNC (Distribution Numerical Control), WMS (Warehouse Management System), and SCADA (Supervisory Control and Data Acquisition), etc., the implementation method of personalized data display GUI is discussed as well. The study is based on the KMMES developed by Wuhan KM-Software of China, and it has been deployed in over forty companies from the sections of aerospace, automotive, shipbuilding and other industries.

Keywords: MES · Integration · Interoperability · Data security access · Intelligent manufacturing

1 Introduction

The application of Industry 4.0 technology can help to establish smart factories and virtual production systems in optimized and competitive features. Along with the latest technologies development, the existing mass batch manufacturing mode will be changed to large-scale personalized production mode but is affordable. It means that the production mode innovation will change the market competition manner, i.e., from price competition to comprehensive quality competition. MES is one of the indispensable systems for building an industrial software layer of such smart factories and

S. Dupuy-Chessa and H. A. Proper (Eds.): CAiSE 2020 Workshops, LNBIP 382, pp. 41–52, 2020.
https://doi.org/10.1007/978-3-030-49165-9_4

the virtual production systems. It plays a bridge role between ERP, DNC and the other systems in the entire manufacturing system.

According to the Industry 4.0 technology, an intelligent manufacturing system to a five layers architecture can be inferred as below, i.e., the underlying is automation equipment layer; the second is the information physical system layer; the third is the industrial software layer; the fourth is the enterprise operations and management layers, and the top layer is the enterprise management optimization layer. In the architecture, the MES belongs to the third layer, i.e., the industrial software layer. By integrating with ERP to obtain product design models, manufacturing processes and production planning information, it can provide the necessary data for DNC, WMS, SCADA, and the other related systems in the workshop. It means that the operating efficiency and performance of the automated production system will be greatly affected if the integration of MES and related systems cannot be solved properly. Therefore, MES integration problems can be transformed into data interoperability management between MES and related business systems.

The current research on MES mainly focused on the following aspects: (1) MES and manufacturing system hardware integration [1, 2, 9–11], aimed to solve the problem of MES management of workshop manufacturing resources; (2) MES industry applications and related software system integration [3, 4, 8], such as the integration of MES and ERP; (3) with the development of intelligent manufacturing technology, the status, functions and integration platforms of MES in intelligent manufacturing systems issues have gradually become research hotspots [6, 7, 9–12], including vertical integration of manufacturing assets (i.e., supporting virtual production line evaluation by simulation) and horizontal integration (i.e., cloud manufacturing); (4) the standards and specifications to support MES integration [13, 14]. Therefore, in a broad sense, in-depth research on MES integration objects and integration scope of data interoperability is still lacking or insufficient, especially in the researches on how to incorporate data access security issues in the MES integration architecture.

Therefore, the research objectives/questions are: how to establish a more comprehensive MES data interoperability object model, incorporate the distributed data security access mechanism with the MES integration architecture, and then apply the solution in discrete manufacturing sector.

2 The Related Work

According to ISO/IEC 2382-01, the definition of data interoperability in the basic terminology of information technology is as follows: to require users to have little or no knowledge of the unique characteristics of these functional units, establish communication mechanisms in each functional unit and execute the ability to program or transfer data. The related work on MES interoperability mainly normally includes MES integration specification and MES integration development. The following are briefly discussed.

2.1 Specifications for MES Integration

In supporting MES integration and data interoperability, the popular specifications and standards are ISA-95 and the SPL (Process Specification Language) proposed by the American NIST, and the integration specifications proposed by MES developers for some specific applications. ISA-95 (IEC/ISO 62246 standard) defines a comprehensive set of functional models, which can reflect the organizational functional architecture of an enterprise and can be extended to meet the needs of different integrations [13]. In terms of manufacturing processes, to solve the problem of interoperability of process information, the United States NIST proposed a PSL (Process Specification Language) specification [14]. In terms of MES modeling technology, Witsch [5] developed a novel MES modeling language (MES-ML), which integrates all important and necessary functional views of the MES system; the users can build the interdependence between functional views by MES-ML and then help to create a universal MES system framework model. Thereby it can improve the standardization of the MES software development process.

Aiming at the application integration problem based on the KMPDM platform, our research team developed the user-specific interoperable data display modeling tool based on the KM-software products, i.e., KMPDM/KMCAPP/KMCAD, by expanding the SPL specification [15]. Ultimately, it realized the data integration via XML-based description language.

Based on the above review, the author believes that B2MML (ISA-95) is suitable to describe the information of the production information of MES; PSL can be used for the description of the manufacturing process information, and the user-customized interoperable data display modeling tools we developed in the past can be used for the final MES interoperable data display.

2.2 MES Integration and Development

Earlier, Choi [1] analyzed the MES (Manufacturing Execution System) architecture and explored how to integrate with the FMS (Flexible Manufacturing System) production line in an ERP (Enterprise Planning System) environment, similar to the current MES and Manufacturing system integration issues, in which a two-layer MES architecture was proposed. To further solve the hardware integration problem of the distributed manufacturing systems, Garetti [2] used an integration method based on Ontology and Web services technology to propose a new type of automated manufacturing system control architecture solution, which allowed the control system to be easily implemented, including configuration, update, and extending. This integrated method provided a completely open environment for the operation and control of the manufacturing assets and could easily and quickly troubleshoot the manufacturing system of a new factory.

MES is also applied in continued manufacturing sections, e.g., iron and steel industry. For example, Li [3] proposed a three-tier automation system integration scheme based on BPS (Business Planning System)/MES/PCS (Process Control System). The comprehensive functions of this MES were analyzed in detail and were applied in Shanghai Iron and Steel Company. In terms of PLM and MES integration, due to the large differences in the integrated data format, source, scale, etc., Anis [4] proposed to integrate a product design, manufacturing system hardware data, and real-time data generated in the production process to design an intermediary system that resolves syntactic and semantic conflicts. In the integration of various functions within the MES, Jeon [8] introduced a design method of advanced MES (i.e., intelligent MES), by establishing a collaboration mechanism of MES internal functions. It supported the functions improvement and auxiliary management decision-making capability of the MES in data collection and analysis. Anyway, it only analyzed its feasibility by simulation based on the established TO-BE scenario model and AS-IS model.

With the development of Industry 4.0 technology, the status, role and integration methods of MES in intelligent manufacturing systems have also become research hotspots. For example, Novak [6] believes that intelligent manufacturing systems can use a five-layer pyramid to describe an automated system structure. To support dynamic production scheduling, provide the flexibility of intelligent manufacturing systems, and reduce response time, it presented a way to integrate a production planning and scheduling module within MES. However, the levels and integration methods of software such as DNC/CAPP are not concerned. Cai [7] aimed at the integration of the distributed manufacturing services in virtual factories, and adopted the ontology and constraint-based distributed manufacturing service modeling methods to develop a prototype of the semantic Web system of ManuHub (i.e., Manufacturing Center), which provides a friendly graphical user interface to search for the required services and get the semantic annotations for the manufacturing assets services. Ghielmini [9] and Mourtzis [10] believes that the existing ICT solutions have low interoperability in supporting the distributed manufacturing assets integration for small and medium enterprises. Therefore, they proposed a virtual factory framework (VFF) to solve this problem, including semantic shared data models, virtual factory managers (VFM), and so on. Mourtzis [11] proposed an integrated quality monitoring method to support cloud manufacturing in virtual factories. Iarovyi [12] proposed an open, knowledge-driven MES architecture by adopting the base-of-breed method, which can effectively support MES to intelligently expand functions and performance, improve MES application quality, and reduce configuration costs and system downtime.

In summary, according to the aforementioned review, in-depth research on MES integration objects and integration scope of data interoperability is still lacking. In particular, research on how to incorporate the data access security mechanism in MES is also inadequate. Therefore, our research should focus on how to establish a comprehensive MES data interoperability object model, introduce the data security access module with MES data interoperability, and ultimately establish a feasible MES integration framework for discrete manufacturing.

3   Methodology

By comprehensively analyzing the strengths and weaknesses of the existing MES integration and its development technologies, the author believes that starting from analyzing the input and output of MES interoperable objects to establish the MES data interoperable object model is feasible and reasonable.

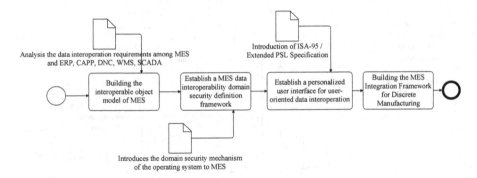

Fig. 1. Proposed modeling methodology

Then to integrate data access security measures with MES data, it can be used to establish an MES integration framework that is more suitable for the actual application requirements of discrete manufacturing (such as machining workshops) and develop applications verification by referring to the principal of the domain-based security mechanism of the operating system. The concept of domain here can be defined according to the user's department, role, etc., and the business domain of MES user can be distinguished as well as the corresponding authority. Therefore, the domain is a key concept in MES data interoperability security management. It takes the method of pre-defining the access rights of personnel at different levels and roles in the virtual manufacturing system. The applied methodology is illustrated in Fig. 1.

When establishing the MES interoperability object model, it is necessary to fully investigate the data interoperation types, input and output information, and processes of MES and ERP, CAPP, DNC, WMS, SCADA systems; and then to use the principle of operating system domain security mechanisms to establish a hierarchical architecture of users secure access to the domain data. Furthermore, using the ISA-95/extended PSL specification (application of B2MML to describe production information and extended PSL to describe process information) and the user-oriented personalized data inter-operable access interface definition tool, a complete MES integration framework for the data interoperability can be established.

4 Proposed Integration Architecture

According to the above section, the exploration of interoperation data object modeling, the discussion of the data interoperable secure access modules based on domain security mechanisms, and the exploration of user-oriented data interoperable person-alized interface development methods will be carried out successively as the following.

4.1 Data Interoperation Object Modeling

According to the investigation result of data interoperation type, input and output of MES and ERP, CAPP, DNC, WMS, SCADA systems, the MES data interoperation object model are established as Fig. 2.

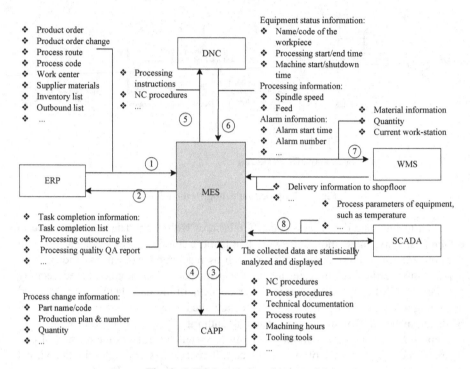

Fig. 2. MES integration object model

Among them, the main input and output information is as follows. (1) MES is responsible for receiving planning instruction information issued from the upstream ERP (Enterprise Resource Planning) system, i.e., how many products are completed at what time; products information is also sent to MES, i.e., what the products needed to manufacturing, including products function specification, size, material, etc. (2) MES feeds back the relevant information about the production and the progress of component manufacturing process execution to ERP. (3) The CAPP system sends the products manufacturing methods, processes, and the required types of manufacturing assets (such as machine tools and equipment, etc.) to the MES, i.e., how the products are processed, the processing steps and their operations and the required processes equipment (e.g., tools, fixtures, gauges, and accessories, etc.). (4) MES will feedback on the execution status of the parts processing to CAPP so that the process planners can refer to the execution information of the process task when they design new manufacturing processes or execute processes change design. (5) The MES sends the CNC machining instructions in the CAM to the DNC system according to the production plan, and then the DNC system downloads the cutting program to the CNC machine. (6) DNC needs to feedback the equipment information to the MES (information of the parts being processed by the machine tool, processing status, processing start time and estimated end time). (7) The MES sends the materials and quantity information of the currently processed parts to the WMS. After the processing is completed, it is stored in the warehouse and the completed part information is entered into WMS/ERP. (8) MES interacts with SCADA. On the one hand, when the MES is scheduled for production, it is necessary to obtain the status of manufacturing assets from SCADA (whether the equipment is normal, whether the operators are on the job, whether the inventory is sufficient, etc.), and pass the processing parameters to the processing equipment and testing equipment; on the other hand, MES sends statistical analysis data of workshop equipment to the SACADA and then the management staff can access the information by graphical viewing tools.

4.2   Domain-Based Data Access Security

The application of MES in the distributed manufacturing mode needs to provide a secure access mechanism to the data of all parties to meet the privacy protection requirements of the group's distributed applications. In this designed security mechanism, the system can use the "domain" to identify the organization's access scope to the individual data, and users belonging to the current organization are allowed to access the current domain data. If domain users need to access data in other domains, it needs to grant the users who need cross-domain access through the system administrator to realize.

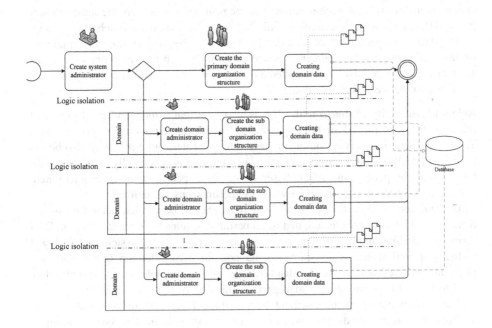

Fig. 3. Domain-based data security policy definition process

Usually, there is only one "primary domain" in the system, and the system administrator has the administrative rights of the primary domain. The domains that the system administrator creates later are all subdomains, and users in the subdomains can only access data in their private domains. The system administrator can access the data of all sub-domains as required. The domain-based data security policy definition process is shown in above Fig. 3.

Main Domain and System Administrator. After logging in to the main domain, the system administrator can perform domain-related operations and manage subdomains and related activities. These include:

(1) Add, modify, and delete the subdomains, i.e., creating subdomain, naming administrator of the subdomain.
(2) Browse and management subdomain. However, under normal circumstances, the primary domain administrator should not directly manipulate the subdomain data, but only manage the subdomain and its organization, and the subdomain administrator and users manage the corresponding data.
(3) Check and manage the logged-in users of the MES, and intervene in the management of operations that do not meet the private data access management requirements.
(4) Modify the configuration and metadata definitions belonging to the main domain.

Only the system administrator of the primary domain is a superuser. The other organizational users' data access authority in the primary domains are the same as users in the subdomains. Usually, they can only log in to the domain to which they belong.

The data in a specific subdomain can be manually specified by the system administrator, and users in other domains can access them through the pre-defined processes and tasks. This mechanism is also called a data sharing policy, which can support work collaboration between multiple domains.

Role and Authority Management. Role is a concept that is independent of users and refers to the role played in the organization of the corresponding responsibilities. Therefore, users in an organization can have multiple roles, but a role may also be the attribute of multiple users. However, only when the role is specifically associated with the user can the permissions of the "user + role" in a specific domain be determined, and the domain should be specified when the permissions are defined.

Domain and its data access permission rules should be created according to the domain in which they are created, that is, all permission rules have a clear domain. Data access permissions and function usage permissions created by the system are displayed in the graphical interface according to the domain. Cross-domain permissions are physically isolated and cannot be displayed directly in the subdomain. Instead, they need to be accessed through the management function of the main domain.

The system authority management adopts three layers of management: system administrator, security administrator, and security log auditor. The system administrator, security administrator, and security log auditor are three independent roles with different responsibilities, namely: the system administrator is responsible for creating and defining the domain organization structure and associated the roles with the personnel, of which the primary domain administrator is only responsible for the subdomain management, and normally the subdomain administrator is responsible for the management of the subdomain's organizational structure. The system security

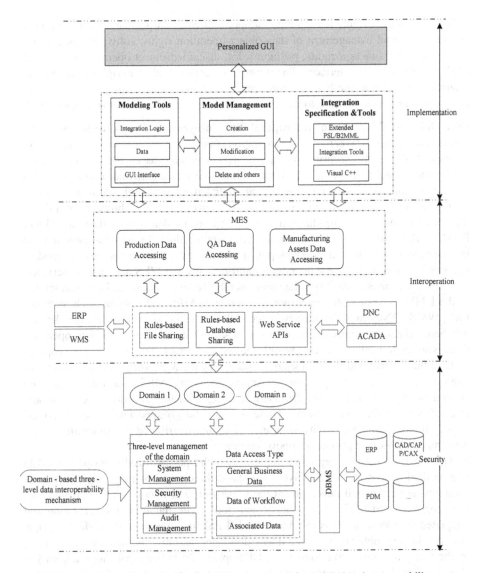

Fig. 4. User-oriented integration hierarchy model for MES data interoperability

administrator defines data access rights and management functions for users in the domain according to data access requirements; the security log auditor is responsible for the security issued to the system abnormal log management, tracking rectification, and ensuring the data access security for the entire distributed collaborative work environment (Fig. 4).

The data access rights management adopts a hierarchical strategy, which supports the definition and management of data object operation rights, software function use rights, extended function rights, position roles, discarded object operation rights, and attribute authorization interfaces. The information about level-level rights management is stored according to the tree structure, and the tree nodes are displayed according to the domain in which they are located, achieving hierarchical management and control.

User-Oriented MES Data Interoperability Integration Framework. First, the foundation (bottom layer) of the integration framework is the security layer. As mentioned above, the security mechanism uses a domain-based three-layer security management mechanism, that is, a system administrator, a security administrator, and a security log auditor. Data access requests are initiated by users in the domain. Through the top-level data interoperability integration framework interoperability layer, a three-layer secure data access mechanism and DBMS are used to obtain data from ERP, PDM, CAD/CAPP/CAX, and other related systems; then through the personalized interface implementation layer development tool can establish the data display models required by users and provide them with multi-dimensional MES data display services.

The second layer is the MES data interoperability layer. In our earlier development of the KMMES system, the interoperation mode of MES and systems such as PDM, ERP, WMS, DNC, SCADA mainly adopted the three modes: rule-based file sharing, rule-based database sharing, and web service-based data shared. The interoperation framework is logically isolated through the work domain. The data access scope of users in the domain and the data sharing strategy of the MES (intra-domain sharing or cross-domain sharing) are predefined. Among them, the MES data access types are general business data, relevant data created along with the workflow execution, and data affected by data associations. These data can be grouped into three categories, namely production data, quality assurance data, and distributed manufacturing assets data (machine tools, equipment, robots, operators, etc.).

The top level of the integration framework is the personalized interoperation data display deployment layer. This layer consists of three parts, namely: integrated specifications and integrated development tools, personalized data display GUI modeling tools, personalized GUI model management tools. The integration specification and integrated development tools provide extended PSL language and B2MML language, describe the data obtained from the interaction layer, and display the data after parsing by the software tools. In the toolkit, a GUI graphical definition dynamic link library is also developed by Visual C++ which supports the encapsulation for the common controls, so that users can easily define the personalized GUI by drag and drop, including text boxes, dialog boxes, buttons, etc. The personalized data display GUI modeling tool supports logic modeling, GUI interface layout design, and GUI control and data association definition. The model management tool provides personalized GUI model creation, modification, deletion, and other operations.

After defining the personalized data display GUI through the deployment tool of the implementation layer, users can browse the predefined data through the MES GUI. If the corresponding permissions are defined, the required data can also be edited and deleted.

5 Conclusion and Future Work

MES, which focuses on the integrated management of distributed manufacturing resources, is facing how to integrate these resources and how to perform data interoperation with related software systems. The research starts with the establishment of an MES data interoperability object model and discusses the types of data interoperability, input and output information, and processes of MES and ERP, CAPP, DNC, WMS, and SCADA systems; proposes a three-level data security access mechanism by the system administrators, security management and security log auditors, which not only supports data security access for users in the domain but also provides cross-domain data sharing rule definitions to support distributed business collaboration. The integrated framework modeling method was applied in KMMES developed by Wuhan KM-Soft Co., and more than 40 sets were deployed in aerospace, automotive, shipbuilding and other sections.

To better support the virtual factory application system, next, we will continue to research on how MES integrates virtual factory horizontal and vertical integration technology, optimize the production plans of the distributed MES, and improve the management level of virtual manufacturing assets.

Acknowledgment. This project is funded by the State Key Research and Development Program of China (2017YFE0118700); and received funding from the European Union's Horizon 2020 research and innovation programme under the Marie Skłodowska-Curie grant agreement No 734599.

References

1. Choi, B.K., Kim, B.H.: MES (manufacturing execution system) architecture for FMS compatible to ERP (enterprise planning system). Int. J. Comput Integr Manuf **15**(3), 274–284 (2002)
2. Garetti, M., Fumagalli, L., Lobov, A., Lastra, J.L.M.: Open automation of manufacturing systems through integration of ontology and web services. In: IFAC Proceedings Volumes, vol. 46, no. 9, pp. 198–203 (2013)
3. Li, H., Pang, X., Zheng, B., Chai, T.: The architecture of manufacturing execution system in iron & steel enterprise. In: IFAC Proceedings Volumes, vol. 38, no. 1, pp. 181–186 (2005)
4. Anis, K., Sébastien, H., Abdelaziz, B.: Integration between MES and product lifecycle management. In: IEEE International Conference on Emerging Technologies and Factory Automation (2011). https://doi.org/10.1109/etfa.2011.6058993
5. Witsch, M., Vogel-Heuser, B.: Towards a formal specification framework for manufacturing execution systems. IEEE Trans. Ind. Inform. **8**(2), 311–320 (2012)
6. Novák, P., Vyskočil, J., Kadera, P.: Plan executor mes: manufacturing execution system combined with a planner for Industry 4.0 production systems. In: Mařík, V., et al. (eds.) HoloMAS 2019. LNCS (LNAI), vol. 11710, pp. 67–80. Springer, Cham (2019). https://doi.org/10.1007/978-3-030-27878-6_6
7. Cai, M., Zhang, W.Y., Zhang, K.: ManuHub: a semantic web system for ontology-based service management in distributed manufacturing environments. IEEE Trans. Syst. Man and Cybern. - Part A: Syst. Humans **41**(3), 574–582 (2011)

8. Jeon, B.W., Um, J., Yoon, S.C., Suk-Hwan, S.: J. Comput.-Aided Design Appl. **14**(4), 472–485 (2017). https://doi.org/10.1080/16864360.2016.1257189

9. Ghielmini, G., Pedrazzoli, P., Rovere, D., et al.: Virtual factory manager for semantic data handling. CIRP J. Manuf. Sci. Technol. **6**(4), 281–291 (2013)

10. Mourtzis, D., Milas, N., Athinaios, N.: Towards Machine 4.0: general machine model for CNC machines through OPC-UA. CIRP **78**, 301–306 (2018)

11. Mourtzis, D., Vlachou, E.: Cloud-based cyber physical systems and quality of services. TQM Emerald J. **28**(5), 704–733 (2016)

12. Iarovyi, S., Xu, X., Lobov, A., Martinez Lastra, J.L., Strzelczak, S.: Architecture for open, knowledge-driven manufacturing execution system. In: Umeda, S., Nakano, M., Mizuyama, H., Hibino, H., Kiritsis, D., von Cieminski, G. (eds.) APMS 2015. IAICT, vol. 460, pp. 519–527. Springer, Cham (2015). https://doi.org/10.1007/978-3-319-22759-7_60

13. Unver, H.O.: An ISA-95-based manufacturing intelligence system in support of lean initiatives. Int. J. Adv. Manuf. Technol. **65**(5–8), 853–866 (2012)

14. Schlenoff, C., Gruninger M., Tissot, F., et al.: The Process Specification Language (PSL): overview and Version 1.0 specification. NISTIR 6459, National Institute of Standards and Technology, Gaithersburg, MD (2000)

15. Zhang, J., Zhou, H., Chen, Z., Yan, X.: A model driven approach for developing PDM-based integrated systems. In: ISCID, vol. 2, pp. 532–535 (2009)

Towards Smart Manufacturing with Dynamic Dataspace Alignment

Donatella Firmani[1]([email]), Francesco Leotta[2], Federica Mandreoli[3],
and Massimo Mecella[2]

[1] Università Roma Tre, Rome, Italy
donatella.firmani@uniroma3.it
[2] Sapienza Università di Roma, Rome, Italy
{leotta,mecella}@diag.uniroma1.it
[3] Università di Modena e Reggio Emilia, Modena, Italy
federica.mandreoli@unimore.it

Abstract. The technological foundation of smart manufacturing consists of cyber-physical systems and the Internet-of-Things (IoT). Despite *smart manufacturing* has become a key paradigm to promote the integration of manufacturing processes using digital technologies, the manufacturing processes themselves are designed by human experts in a traditional way and have limited ability to adapt their behavior to exceptional circumstances. We leverage the fact that each IoT device in a smart factory can be coupled with a *digital twin* – that is, a software artefact that faithfully represents the physical system using real-time sensor data – to envision a software architecture to support adaptation of the manufacturing process when divergence from reference practices occur.

Keywords: Smart manufacturing · Digital Twins · Internet-of-Things

1 Introduction

Production processes are nowadays fragmented across different companies and organized in global multi-tier supply chains. This is the result of a first wave of globalization, fueled by the diffusion of Internet-based Information and Communication Technologies in the early years 2000. The recent wave of new Industry 4.0 technologies is further multiplying opportunities, with a wide range of services offered by small and medium-sized suppliers and automated production plants routinely employing thousands of devices from hundreds of vendors.

In such a dynamic context, *smart manufacturing* has become a key paradigm, using digital technologies to promote the integration of product design processes, manufacturing processes, and general collaborative business processes across factories and enterprises. Smart factories consist of a multi-layered integration of the information related to various activities along the factory and related resources. However, processes still generally reflect established work practices and have limited ability to properly adapt their behavior to exceptional circumstances where variations or divergence from reference practices occur.

© Springer Nature Switzerland AG 2020
S. Dupuy-Chessa and H. A. Proper (Eds.): CAiSE 2020 Workshops, LNBIP 382, pp. 53–58, 2020.
https://doi.org/10.1007/978-3-030-49165-9_5

Example 1. Consider a cardboard manufacturing scenario where two types of die cutters are available, dubbed type 1 and type 2, with different digital communication interfaces, potentially adopting a different language and vocabulary, and employed in two separate production processes. Suppose that a customer makes a new order for type 1 while type 1 die cutters are busy processing a former order. The cardboard manufacturer can either wait until type 1 become idle again and possibly miss its production goal or re-configure a type 2 die cutter (if available) to serve as a substitute. Such interoperability is a critical goal for the cardboard manufacturer to avoid interruptions in the production process, but traditional manual mapping and configuration practices take time and anticipating all possible scenarios at design-time is often infeasible.

In smart factories, physical devices typically have a faithful representation in the digital world, usually referred to as *digital twins*. A Digital Twin (DT) exposes a set of *services* allowing to execute certain operations and produce data describing its activity. DTs are typically used to query or manipulate the state of the shop floor and the availability of DT data can have a huge impact on the design of manufacturing processes. We can imagine shop floor data stored in a factory *data space* together with other information, e.g., data available from the company's employment and production history, business data and worker preferences. Such information in the data space can be used to allow agility of the manufacturing process and even automatic composition of the intermediate steps for achieving a production goal, for instance by suggesting a specific mapping for automatic configuration of the type 2 die cutter in the example above.

Our final aim is to support *agile recovery* of smart manufacturing processes at run-time when unanticipated events in the industrial practices occur. Our goal is to automatically detect variations with respect to reference practices and trigger the exploration of the factory data space to discover the needed services and data, thus requiring no specification of policies at design-time to handle all possible events. It is worth mentioning that the EFFRA association identifies "agile value networks" as one of the five key priorities for the Future of Factories to deliver innovative products with a high degree of personalization.

Our Contribution. In this paper we discuss available technologies that can be used to achieve our final goal and describe how a user can leverage the adaptive architecture for smart manufacturing described in [4]. The considered architecture captures indeed analogies between DTs and traditional software services (accessible for instance through Web technologies) and enables automatic integration and composition of DTs through data available in the data space.

2   Background and Related Work

Authors in [12] provide an overview of Industry 4.0 features in multiple reference architectures and develops a maturity model for IT architectures for data-driven manufacturing. The group around Reference Architecture Model Industry 4.0 – RAMI – developed a detailed conceptual architecture and a first implementation of the digital twin, the open Asset Administrative Shell. RAMI still does not pursue a seamless integrated approach, which starting from processes arrives to data nor supports in-process dynamic orchestration of services and data. Authors in [3] provide a methodological and technological support to agile supply chains in the Industry 4.0 context. To this end, it sets forth an architectural framework that leverages RAMI 4.0 and addresses the methodological issue of making RAMI 4.0 capable of enabling agility in supply chains. In this paper, Business Process Management (BPM) is proposed as a mean to coordinate all the different actors of a digital factory, but no exploration policies of the data available in the factory data space are considered.

Digital Twins. Although the concept of DT dates back to 2002 [6], DTs gained popularity among researchers and practitioners only recently, with the spread of IoT technologies. Authors in [1] introduce a DT reference model for a cloud-based cyber-physical system (such as a smart city) based on a smart interaction controller using a Bayesian belief network. They provide a context-based control decision scheme that uses Bayesian networks and fuzzy logic based rules to select any of these system modes for inter-system interactions. Authors in [13] introduce a novel architecture for large-scale DT platforms including a distributed DT cooperation framework, flexible data-centric communication middleware, and the platform-based DT application to develop a reliable advanced driver assistance system. Finally, the work of [11] provides a conceptual model and specific operation mechanisms for a DT *shop-floor*, that is, a basic unit of manufacturing, where data from both physical and virtual sides as well as the fused data are provided to drive all the steps of the production process. For sake of completeness, we also mention the concepts of Digital Shadow (DS) and Digital Model (DM). While in DTs the state of the physical object can affect the state of the digital object and vice-versa, (i) in DSs only the state of the physical object can affect the state of the digital object, and (ii) in DMs the state of the digital object is computed via simulation. We refer the reader to [8] for more discussion.

Polystores. In digital factories, it is of strategic importance to provide effective mechanisms for searching information along diverse and distributed data sources. Data interoperability and integration techniques have been proposed as a way for resolving the structural and semantic heterogeneities that can exist between data stored in distinct repositories. However, such techniques can be difficult to implement for the many organizations deploying polyglot architectures with different data management systems [7]. Polystores [10], together with its first reference implementation BigDAWG [5] have been proposed recently as a valuable solution for this scenario. A polystore system provides a loosely coupled integration over multiple, disparate data models and query languages. In this system, queries are posed over *islands of information*, i.e. collections of data sources, each accessed with a single query language, and the same data can be accessed from multiple islands. The issue of data manipulation in polystores has been addressed in different papers. In [9], the authors propose the introduction of a probabilistic relation that allows the enrichment of query answering with data outside the queried data source but available in the polystore (Fig. 1).

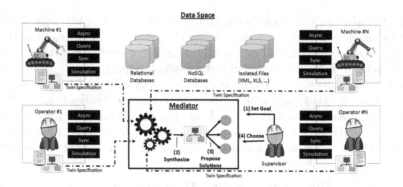

Fig. 1. The smart manufacturing architecture described in [4].

3 Architectural Model

We now summarize the main features of the architecture in [4] and discuss how it can be used for the purpose of agile recovery of smart manufacturing processes.

DTs wrap physical entities involved in the process. These physical entities can be manufacturing machines or human operators. A DT exposes a Web API consisting, in general, of three parts: the synchronous one, the query interface and the asynchronous one. The synchronous interface allows to give instructions to the physical entity. These instructions may, for example, produce a state change in a manufacturing machine (in case the twin is over a machine) or ask a human operator to perform a manual task (in case the twin is over a manufacturing worker). The query interface allows for asking information to the physical entity about its state and accessing the related data (possibly by applying diagnostic and prognostic functions results of machine learning). The asynchronous interface generates events available to subscribers.

The data space contains all the data available to the process. These data are heterogeneous in their nature from the access technology point of view, the employed schema (or its absence) and the employed vocabulary. It is important to note how the DTs contribute to the data space with both the query API and the asynchronous one. Other sources for the data space may include relational and no-SQL databases or unstructured sources which constitute the factory information system. In the approach in [4], the data space can be modelled as a polystore. We inherit the data modelling approach proposed in [9] where a polystore is made of a set of databases stored in a variety of data management systems, each one potentially offered by a twin through the query interface.

The human supervisor is the one defining the goals of the process in terms of both final outcomes and key performance indicators to be obtained.

The Recovery Task. Upon unanticipated events resulting in variations with respect to reference practices, available DTs and data must be integrated. This task is fulfilled by the mediator. The mediator acts in two phases: the *synthesis phase* and the *execution/recovery phase*. During the synthesis phase, the specifications of the APIs exposed by digital twins and the meta-data (e.g. data source schemas) available in the data space, are composed in order to construct a *mediator process*. During the execution/recovery phase, the mediator run his program and detects possible variations with respect to reference practices (such as, the presence of a type 2 die cutter as a substitute of a type 1 die cutter in Example 1). Detection can be done by using situation calculus to model the manufacturing process, sending a run-time alert when there is no further step available in the process and identifying the DTs involved in the anomaly (such as, type 2 die cutter in Example 1). Upon detection of a variation, the mediator can perform the recovery task by composing the required input/output messages requested by the anomalous DTs and thus integrating them into the regular manufacturing process. To this end, the mediator can explore the factory data space, translate and integrate the data available to comply with the format requested by the DTs involved in the recovered sequencing/interleaving. A technique for exploring data spaces modelled a polystore is described in [9]. In this context, DTs can be modeled as guarded automaton [2]: the synchronous API of the DT corresponds to input messages of the guarded automaton and the data contained in the local storage is part of the polystore defining the process.

4   Concluding Remarks

In this paper, we describe our preliminary effort towards an approach to automatically recover a smart manufacturing process at run-time, through automatic discovery of the needed services and data. To this end, we discussed available technologies that can be used to achieve this goal and how an adaptive architecture for smart manufacturing, based on the notion of Digital Twin (DT) can be used effectively. Our approach supports agile supply chains through innovative technological solutions aiming at the dynamic discovery of service and data flows that best fit the requirements expressed in smart manufacturing process specifications and their evolution. Next steps include developing frameworks for real manufacturing machines and company services. To this end, we are conducting a real world study in a cardboard manufacturing scenario.

Acknowledgments. This work has been partly supported by the European Commission through the H2020 project *FIRST – virtual Factories: Interoperation suppoRting buSiness innovaTion* (grant agreement # 734599). The work of Francesco Leotta and Massimo Mecella has been also partly supported by the research contract with Rota Laser Dies.

References

1. Alam, K.M., El Saddik, A.: C2PS: a digital twin architecture reference model for the cloud-based cyber-physical systems. IEEE Access **5**, 2050–2062 (2017)
2. Berardi, D., Calvanese, D., De Giacomo, G., Hull, R., Mecella, M.: Automatic composition of transition-based semantic web services with messaging. In: Proceedings of the 31st International Conference on Very Large Data Bases, pp. 613–624, VLDB Endowment (2005)

3. Bicocchi, N., Cabri, G., Mandreoli, F., Mecella, M.: Dynamic digital factories for agile supply chains: an architectural approach. J. Ind. Inf. Integr. **15**, 111–121 (2019)
4. Catarci, T., Firmani, D., Leotta, F., Mandreoli, F., Mecella, M., Sapio, F.: A conceptual architecture and model for smart manufacturing relying on service-based digital twins. In: 2019 IEEE International Conference on Web Services, ICWS 2019, Milan, Italy, 8–13 July 2019, pp. 229–236 (2019)
5. Duggan, J., et al.: The BigDAWG polystore system. ACM SIGMOD Rec. **44**(2), 11–16 (2015)
6. Grieves, M.W.: Virtually intelligent product systems: digital and physical twins. In: Complex Systems Engineering: Theory and Practice, pp. 175–200 (2019)
7. Kadadi, A., Agrawal, R., Nyamful, C., Atiq, R.: Challenges of data integration and interoperability in big data. In: 2014 IEEE International Conference on Big Data (Big Data), pp. 38–40. IEEE (2014)
8. Kritzinger, W., Karner, M., Traar, G., Henjes, J., Sihn, W.: Digital twin in manufacturing: a categorical literature review and classification. IFAC-PapersOnLine **51**(11), 1016–1022 (2018)
9. Maccioni, A., Torlone, R.: Augmented access for querying and exploring a polystore. In: Proceedings of the 34th IEEE International Conference on Data Engineering, ICDE, pp. 77–88 (2018)
10. Stonebraker, M.: The case for polystores (2015). https://wp.sigmod.org/?p=1629
11. Tao, F., Zhang, M.: Digital twin shop-floor: a new shop-floor paradigm towards smart manufacturing. IEEE Access **5**, 20418–20427 (2017)
12. Weber, C., Königsberger, J., Kassner, L., Mitschang, B.: M2DDM - a maturity model for data-driven manufacturing. Procedia CIRP **63**, 173–178 (2017)
13. Yun, S., Park, J.H., Kim, W.T.: Data-centric middleware based digital twin platform for dependable cyber-physical systems. In: 2017 Ninth International Conference on Ubiquitous and Future Networks (ICUFN), pp. 922–926. IEEE (2017)

ISESL 2020

ISESL 2020 Preface

In the era of digitalization, new technologies (augmented reality, cyber-physical systems, networks, cloud computing, social media, and so on) change not only enterprises and organizations functioning, but also all aspects of human life: healthcare, cities governance, agriculture, robots, tourism, ecological trends... the list can be long. These various technologies are intended to improve or enhance the life of human beings. In one way or another, they intend to contribute to a smarter life.

Until now, digital technologies have been brought into the game as silo solutions, mostly for themselves and efficiency as the main purpose. Reasoning holistically about information in the context of a bank or a manufacturing plant is routine practice. However, it is less common with emerging technologies for everyday life public digital application. We deeply believe that methods, models, and techniques inherited from information systems engineering research could considerably improve the way human interact with the digital world and would enhance the user experience to live a smarter life.

The goal of the workshop is to bring together researchers and practitioners who are interested in the application of disruptive approaches to foster a smarter life. The workshop topics include, but are not limited to, the application and emerging concepts of rising digital technologies to different fields of life through ICT (information communication technology). This holistic approach, mixing human life and digital systems, is a challenge for the 21st century and society.

For this first edition of the ISESL workshop, we selected 6 contributions (4 full and 2 short papers) from 12 submitted papers, and invited 1 paper. The review process was single blind. Each paper was reviewed by three or four Program Committee members. The invited paper introduces a new concept: Artificial Sentience that complements artificial intelligence to drive digital technology towards consciousness. The three following papers deal with information systems engineering applications to various aspects of human life: healthcare, agriculture, and tourism. The next three papers address fields of society management: social participation networks, sustainability, and governance.

We thank all authors of the submitted papers for their contribution to the ISESL 2020 workshop. We are grateful to all Program Committee members and the organizers of the CAiSE 2020 conference for trust and support.

April 2020

Elena Kornyshova
Eric Gressier Soudan
John Murray

ISESL 2020 Organization

Workshop Chairs

Elena Kornyshova   Conservatoire National des Arts et Métiers, France
Eric Gressier Soudan Conservatoire National des Arts et Métiers, France
John Murray   San José State University, USA

Program Committee

Said Assar   Institut Mines-Télécom, France
Isabelle Astic   Conservatoire National des Arts et Métiers, France
Marco Bajec   University of Ljubljana, Slovenia
Judith Barrios   University of Los Andes,Venezuela
Nicolas Bouilot   Société des Arts Technologiques, Canada
Sophie Chabridon   Institut Mines-Télécom, France
Raja Chiky   Institut Supérieur d'Electronique de Paris, France
Areti Damala   ENS-CNRS, College de France, France
Rébecca Déneckère   University Paris 1 Panthéon Sorbonne, France
Elena Viorica Epure   Deezer, France
Agnès Front   Université Grenoble Alpes, France
Eric Gressier-Soudan Conservatoire National des Arts et Métiers, France
Gary Graig Hobbs   San José State University, USA
Gérald Kembellec   Institut Historique Allemand, France
Elena Kornyshova   Conservatoire National des Arts et Métiers, France
José Machado   University of Minho, Portugal
Elisabeth Métais   Conservatoire National des Arts et Métiers, France
John Murray   San José State University, USA
Jean-Francois Omhover Microsoft, USA
Pantelis Papadopoulos Aarhus University, Denmark
Oscar Pastor   Universitat Politècnica de València, Spain
Camille Salinesi   University Paris 1 Panthéon Sorbonne, France
Mohammed Sellami   Institut Mines-Télécom, France
Carolyn Talcott   SRI International Menlo Park, USA
Jean Vanderdonckt   Université Catholique de Louvain, Belgium
Gianluigi Viscusi   École Polytechnique Fédérale de Lausanne, Switzerland

The Machine with a Human Face: From Artificial Intelligence to Artificial Sentience

Sylvain Lavelle[1,2(✉)]

[1] ICAM Paris, Centre for Ethics, Technology and Society,
34 Points de Vue, 77127 Lieusaint, France
sylvain.lavelle@icam.fr
[2] Ecole des Hautes Etudes en Sciences Sociales,
54 boulevard Raspail, 75006 Paris, France

Abstract. The main challenge of technology is to facilitate the tasks and to transfer the functions that are usually performed by the humans to the non-humans. However, the pervasion of machines in everyday life requires that the non-humans are increasingly closer in their abilities to the ordinary thought, action and behaviour of the humans. This view merges the idea of the *Humaniter*, a longstanding myth in the history of technology: an artificial creature that thinks, acts and feels like a human to the point that one cannot make the difference between the two. In the wake of the opposition of Strong AI and Weak AI, this challenge can be expressed in terms of a shift from the performance of intelligence (reason, reasoning, cognition, judgment) to that of sentience (experience, sensation, emotion, consciousness). In other words, the challenge of technology if this possible shift is taken seriously is to move from the paradigm of Artificial Intelligence (AI) to that of Artificial Sentience (AS). But for the Humaniter not to be regarded as a mere myth, any intelligent or sentient machine must pass through a Test of Humanity that refers to or that differs from the Turing Test. One can suggest several options for this kind of test and also point out some conditions and limits to the very idea of the Humaniter as an artificial human.

Keywords: Artificial intelligence · Artificial sentience · Humaniter

1 The Myth of the Humaniter

The possible substitution of the machine for the human as regards the mind functions has been the heart of the research program on Artificial Intelligence (AI) since the outset. The idea is to produce an identical or similar performance in a machine for the logical and noetic abilities (from the Greek *logos*, reason, speech, and *noesis*, thought) said wrongly or rightly "superior". There are undoubtedly many possible definitions of AI, and, failing to find a simple and unique one, which covers the whole spectrum of reasoning and cognition, it is nevertheless possible to indicate its objective: "The objective of artificial intelligence is, in the long term, to have everything that man can do in terms of reasoning done by a computer system (Ladrière) [1] ". The fact remains that intelligence, especially if it is artificial, is still the subject of many debates, some

© Springer Nature Switzerland AG 2020
S. Dupuy-Chessa and H. A. Proper (Eds.): CAiSE 2020 Workshops, LNBIP 382, pp. 63–75, 2020.
https://doi.org/10.1007/978-3-030-49165-9_6

going so far as to declare that "Artificial intelligence doesn't exist" [2]. They mean that the substitution of the machine for the human is not so easy and that, rather than an artificial intelligence, it would probably be better to speak of an "enhanced intelligence" [2].

The problem is even more acute when it comes to substituting the machine for the human as regards other functions, sometimes called "inferior" when compared to those of intelligence. More precisely, these are abilities that can be broadly described as empirical and aesthetical (from the Greek *emperia*, experience, and *aisthesis*, sensation). These multiple aptitudes of experience, namely, sensation, perception, emotion and sentiment, to which consciousness can be added, turn attention to the sentience. In this other dimension, perhaps even more complex, of human life lies the origin of a research program which supplements that of artificial intelligence. One could name it, with all the precautions of use, the *Artificial Sentience* (AS), that is to say the exploration and the transfer of the functions and abilities of human experience and senses to a machine. However, it would be legitimate to ask, critically, if it goes for artificial sentience as for artificial intelligence, so that one could state as well that "Artificial sentience doesn't exist" [3][1].

Sentience is a challenge for artificial intelligence, but it can also be presented as its new frontier, and some, like Husain, speak without hesitation of the "sentient machine" [4]. The difficulty of a shift from AI to AS comes from the fact that all human functions and abilities, from the most intellectual to the most sensory, can be transferred to machines. The idea of a total substitution, which concerns both the mind and the body, corresponds to an ancient myth of technology, of the art of production of artefacts and possibly, of artificial creatures [5]. I propose to call it the *Myth of the Humaniter*, that is, the fictitious or imaginary idea of a humanoid artificial creature which allows a total and perfect substitution between human and machine. The Humaniter is an artificial creature which combines and articulates a whole set of human functions and abilities beyond those, more classic, of the Actor or the Producer: the *Reasoner*, for reasoning and intelligence, the *Cogniter,* for knowledge and belief, the *Voliter,* for will and desire, and finally, the *Experiencer,* for experience, sensation, emotion and possibly consciousness. The Humaniter as an artificial creature that replaces the human is held to be a myth, but this does not prevent many researchers from trying to realise it.

The thesis that I would like to defend is the following one: I do not think for a second that the Humaniter can exist, and in particular, that there can be an artificial creature which not only is intelligent, but moreover, can also be sentient. In other words, I think that the Humaniter is indeed a myth and that, just as there is no artificial intelligence, there is no artificial sentience. The major argument in support of this thesis is that, if an artificial creature such as the Humaniter existed, it would be actually a human being. It would be endowed with the same general physical and psychic

---

[1] As Matson stated, "very little, if any, distinctively human or animal behaviourcan be duplicated or possibly simulated by existing machines. No existing machine is sentient, and nothing that any of them could do would go the slightest way toward indicating sentience. But these facts are no interest. We want to talk of possible, conceivable machines", p. 78 .

constitution, and only its creation would be artificial, that is, non-sexual[2]. Nevertheless, I am convinced that, in a certain type of interaction between the human and the machine, it is possible that the machine passes the test of humanity and can be confused with a human.

It is this point that I propose to explore in the second part of this paper, after having presented in the first part what the Humaniter is, considered in its different dimensions, from intelligence to sentience. In this short study, which is only a kind of brief inventory of some aspects of the problem, I propose after formulating the principles to identify certain conditions and limits of each of the options.

2   From Intelligence to Sentience

The Computer as an information and communication machine is at the heart of the research on AI and of the comparison of human and machine for the operations of reasoning and cognition. If one takes the broader paradigm of the Humaniter, it appears that the AS can be viewed as the other side of the transfer of functions and abilities from the human to the machine. However, some questions need to be raised concerning AI and AS, in particular on the difference between the strong version and the weak version and on the question of consciousness.

2.1   From Intelligence to Sentience, Through Consciousness

There are actually various reasons for moving from a research program on intelligence to a research program on sentience. From an operational point of view, it is justified by the need to have machines which, when interacting with humans, behave in a manner that shows their ability to express sensations, emotions and even consciousness. It is a way of making machines more "human", especially if they are called upon to play an increasingly important role in our daily lives. From a reflexive point of view, this shift from intelligence to sentience is justified by the need to better understand the abilities of machines to process information, so that they come as close as possible to the humans processing. This makes it possible to measure the possible difference between the ability of the machine and that of the human and to learn therefore about the singularity of the human, which in turn questions the singularity of the machine [6].

The fact remains that this shift from AI to AS can be interpreted according to the Humaniter's paradigm as an attempt to go through with a substitution of human functions and abilities by the machine. From this point of view, it takes sides, in the debate between strong AI and weak AI, if one takes up the cleavage proposed by Searle, in favour of a strong program, even if it can be shown that only the weak one can be achieved. Strong AI refers to the Artificial Intelligence program which envisions the intelligent machine as endowed with ability not only of reasoning, but also of consciousness. In comparison, weak AI bounds to an intelligent machine deprived from

---

[2] This is an argument which partly links up with the Frankenstein's axiom: "An exact physical replica, although it has been produced, of a sentient being would itself be a sentient being".

this full scope of abilities and that can then function as a device intended to better understand human intelligence, the only one provided with consciousness. One could say that the parallel works for artificial sentience, if we consider that strong AS designates the program of Artificial Sentience in which the sentient machine is endowed with an ability of sensation and emotion and to some extent, consciousness. In comparison, weak AS relates to a sentient machine deprived from this full scope of abilities and that can function as a device intended to better understand human sentience and the role of consciousness.

Now, one can come back to the two principles, the Principle of Artificial Intelligence and the Principle of Artificial Sentience, in order to clarify their meaning, but also, to show their conditions and limits.

2.2   Principle of Artificial Intelligence (AI)

The principle of AI can be formulated as follows:

(1)   *Principle of Artificial Intelligence* (PAI): A machine can think like a human.

From there, you can specify two versions, one strong and the other weak:

(1.a)   *Principle of strong AI*: A machine can think *exactly* like a human, both from the point of view of reasoning and of consciousness.

(1.b)   *Principle of weak AI*: A machine can think *approximately* like a human, both from the point of view of reasoning and of consciousness.

When it is said about a machine that it can think *like* a human, it does not mean the same thing as a machine that thinks *as* a human. Because if it was so, then it would mean that the machine *is* a human who, among other things, is able to say "I" - as in the expression "I think". In this respect, it is illusory to think that when a machine says "I, Robot", it has comparatively the same kind of meaning as in the sentence of a human who says "I, Human"... In addition, it can be noted that the difference between identity ("exactly") and similarity ("approximately") says nothing about the power of reasoning given to the machine by calculation, if only we compare it to that of the human. Thus, a machine can follow a reasoning which approximates that of the human, whereas it is of a power which is clearly higher than that of the human (as in the chess game with Deep Blue, or the Go game with Alpha Go).

Now, it goes without saying that the "thought" has a fairly diverse set of meanings, as suggested by Descartes who uses this term to designate reason, doubt and imagination as well as knowledge, will and sentiment [7][3]. In another interpretation, a philosopher such as Wittgenstein would say that the concept "to think" requires to consider the multiple uses that one makes of it in everyday life, the relationship with language and with the behaviour of the body [8]: "194. We must never forget that 'thinking' is a word of everyday language ... We should not expect him to have a unified use, quite the contrary. 220. 'Thinking' is a largely ramified concept. A concept

---

[3] "Je suis une chose qui pense, c'est-à-dire qui doute, qui affirme, qui nie, qui connaît peu de choses, qui en ignore beaucoup, qui veut, qui ne veut pas, qui imagine aussi, et qui sent ", III.

that contains many manifestations of life. The *phenomena* of thought are dispersed. 223. The expression on the face of someone who thinks, and that of an idiot. The brow that creases in reflection, in attention." This last point raises the whole question of the bodily expression of the mental life, if assumed alike Wittgenstein that it cannot be only "internal". It is, so to speak, its "external" face that draws attention, or more exactly, the coupling of thought with the words of language as well as the behaviour of the body.

A rational approach to the thought suggests that it merges with the different types of reasoning that have been identified in logic. It is customary in this field to differentiate between the reasoning which proceeds by deduction, by induction and by abduction: in other words, going from the general to the particular (syllogism) or from the particular to the general, with in the abduction a return to the particular. However, this implies that certain rules of reasoning stemming from logic are *norms* provided with a binding force for an ordinary reasoning which deviates quite often from them. In contrast, a broader approach to thinking includes, in addition to reasoning, a variety of forms of intelligence, with sometimes an emphasis put on creation and invention, that is, the production of novelty. This is how in a psychological version we distinguish a variety of forms of intelligence, grouped under the expression "multiple intelligence" [9]: the logical-mathematical form, which corresponds to the rational approach; but also, the linguistic, the spatial, the bodily (implementation in dance or sport), the intra-personal (ability to understand oneself) and the inter-personal (ability to understand others), the musical; to these forms can be added the naturalist (ability to recognize animals, plants) and the existential.

However, the term intelligence is taken with caution in psychology, and that of performance is often preferred to it for various fields: execution, adaptation, control, speed of processing, abilities of working memory, of reasoning. Thus, we can see that, even in the research program on artificial intelligence, there is still a long way to go to replace the human with machine. One wonders if the same kind of difficulties occurs in this part of the Humaniter paradigm which makes artificial sentience the other horizon of the research program.

2.3   Principle of Artificial Sentience (AS)

The principle of Artificial Sentience can be formulated as follows:

(2) *Principle of Artificial Sentience* (PAS): A machine can feel like a human.

From there, you can specify two versions, one strong, and the other weak:

(2.a) *Principle of strong AS*: A machine can feel *exactly* like a human, from the point of view of sensation and emotion and of consciousness.

(2.b) *Principle of weak AS*: A machine can feel *approximately* like a human, from the point of view of sensation and emotion and of consciousness.

Again, when it is said that the machine can feel like a human, this view does not imply that it feels *as* a human, as that would imply that it is a human. The significant point is that a human able to say that he or she is a sentient being is a being who has the ability to speak, in particular to say "I", which is linked to an ability to think.

Sentience belongs to the vast realm of "experience" which covers a wide range of meanings, from sensation to sentiment. The nuance as far as the thought is concerned is that experience heard in the sense of phenomenal experience is said in first person, at the risk of fall into Descartes' solipsism. This is suggested by the experiential approach which focuses on phenomenal experience, supposedly distinct from one person to another, since no one can have access to the mental states of others. So, in the sub-jective approach to experience, I have no guarantee that the object as I see it (for example, a squirrel) is seen in the same way by someone else. However, this is a point disputed by Wittgenstein who notes that, by making my experience too much a strictly private matter, it can no longer be identified with that of the others. Yet even the most personal experiences, such as those of sensation and emotion, suppose a public lan-guage and disqualify the idea of a private one used by myself alone in order to express my personal sensation or emotion [8]: "275. Look at the blue of the sky and say to yourself: "How blue the sky is!" If you do it spontaneously - without philosophical intentions - the idea will never occur to you that this impression of colour belongs only to you. And you will have no hesitation in making this exclamation to someone else... 303. Just try to doubt - in a real case - the fear or pain of others!". What the philosopher suggests is such behaviour of doubt, in a real situation, would be for those who suffer perfectly inappropriate and could arouse their greatest anger. This does not detract from the relativity of perception, in the "seeing like" mode, when, in a figure such as the Duck-Rabbit (Jastrow), some see a duck, where others see a rabbit [10].

The field of sentience covers a set of aspects of experience which incite to make a difference between sensation, perception, emotion, sentiment, and in a broad sense, consciousness [11]. Literally, sentience (from the Latin *sentientem*, in the nominative *sentiens*) describes the ability to feel, whereas the gerundive of the verb *sentire* refers to the concept of consciousness, taken in the sense of being aware of what surrounds us. It is common to express the difference in experience between sensation and perception by taking into account what the judgment adds, however basic it may be. This is about how I see an object, for example, a red cube: I have the sensation of the colour red, but I have the perception of a red body as a unit that occupies a certain volume in space. Sensation is distinguished from perception in the sense that my judgment, even at a primitive level, tells me that this object is not just a flat surface. It would then be necessary to add a concept, in this case the concept of "cube", in order to differentiate between a cube and a square, or between a cube and a sphere. Emotion (from the Latin *emovere*, to set in motion) is another dimension of sentience that is not easy to define, perhaps because it covers actually a multitude of aspects. Emotions do have one thing in common, however: they are the subject's overt responses to meaningful events and can trigger distinctive bodily changes and behaviours [12].

2.4   The Question of Consciousness

Consciousness is one of the most difficult problems to solve in any study of both intelligence and sentience, all the more if they are artificial. Numerous studies have attempted to define what consciousness is and to determine whether it is possible that a machine could be endowed with this ability characteristic of humans or certain non-humans (animals). As Chalmers puts it, it is customary to differentiate between "easy problems" and "difficult problems" of consciousness. Easy problems are those which relate to the explanation of cognitive and behavioral functions: for instance, the ability to discriminate, categorize, and react to environmental stimuli; the integration of information by a cognitive system; the reportability of mental states; the ability of a system to access its own internal states; the focus of attention; the deliberate control of behavior; the difference between awakeness and sleep. The difficult problems are those relating to the explanation of conscious experience, whether you call it phenomenal or qualitative if what is insisted on is the *qualia*.

The difficulty of conscious experience is well explained by Chalmers [13]: "the easy problems are easy precisely because they concern the explanation of cognitive *abilities* and *functions*. When it comes to conscious experience, this sort of explanation fails. What makes the hard problem hard and almost unique is that it goes beyond problems about the performance of functions. To see this, note that even when we have explained the performance of all the cognitive and behavioral functions in the vicinity of experience - perceptual discrimination, categorization, internal access, verbal report - there may still remain a further unanswered question: Why is the performance of these functions accompanied by experience? A simple explanation of the functions leaves this question open... This is not to say that experience has no function. Perhaps it will turn out to play an important cognitive role. But for any role it might play, there will be more to the explanation of experience than a simple explanation of the function ... The same criticism applies to any purely physical account of consciousness. For any physical process we specify there will be an unanswered question: Why should this process give rise to experience?".

The question of consciousness, and more specifically, the possibility of an artificial consciousness is as much on the side of artificial intelligence as that of the artificial sentience. But when we take a closer look at the variety of abilities that are grouped under the term "consciousness", it is not surprising that it is found on both sides, as this list shows [14]: attention, creativity, dynamism, emotion, imagination, intelligence, intentionality, language, quality (qualia), perception, self, volition. It follows that the dividing line between intelligence and sentience is not so obvious, especially when you consider the role that consciousness plays in distinguishing between human and machine. This question of consciousness refers more fundamentally to the kind of tests that have been designed to characterize a machine as capable of being endowed with intelligence and sentience.

3   Tests of Humanity

The Humaniter is a machine that, if it is meant to take the place of humans for all or a part of their functions or abilities, must be able to pass a test of humanity. The test of the machine intelligence is now quite well established, even if it continues to generate a lot of debate, but it remains to be clarified what is or what can be a test for the machine sentience. We favour here an approach that insists on the behaviour and the interpretation made of it by a judge, while another approach would rather emphasize the architecture of a system [14][4]. In addition, we favour an approach which, in the wake of the original Turing test, develops a test modality that is not limited to a computer, but results in the action of a machine (a robot), like in the Total Turing Test [15]. It can be suggested that, for intelligence as for sentience, a test of humanity calls upon the criterion of the action of an agent, but without thereby reducing to it the whole of the "human" behaviour of a machine.

3.1 Tests for the Intelligence of a Machine

The Turing Test for the machine intelligence was originally an imitation game which consisted in developing a machine that cannot be distinguished from a human [16]. Turing suggests that a judge J exchanges typed messages with a human being H on the one hand, and a machine M on the other, messages that can relate to all kinds of subjects. Judge J does not know which of his two interlocutors (whom he knows under the names A and B) is the machine M and the human H. In the rules of the game, it is stipulated that, after a series of exchanges, the Judge must guess who between the two of them is respectively the human being and the machine. Correct identification consists for Judge in producing a misidentification rate of 50% identical to what a random answer would give. Turing believes that if a machine one day does not allow correct identification by a human, it is an intelligent machine or, if you put it in other words, a "thinking machine".

The Turing test procedure has given rise to many interesting discussions and is the source of a series of concrete IT achievements, despite the difficulty of a program to pass the Turing test. We can put ourselves in the place of a judge J who dialogues through a computer terminal with the two interlocutors A and B and, from there, identify some possible options. A first option, to recognize the machine, is to ask a question such as "what is the value of 327 at the 4th power?" If A answers 11433811041 after a second and B refuses to answer, or waits a few minutes to propose a result, there is no doubt that A is the machine and B the human. However, the specialists who design the programs for taking the Turing test are not stupid and they foresee this coarse trick. Their program is able to lead the calculation of 327 to the 4th power without difficulty in no time, but it will refuse to answer or ask ten minutes before providing a result, or even offer an incorrect answer. Everything that a human does not fully succeed and that a computer succeeds without difficulty is treated in the same way, by a computer that "pretends" to fail, as if failure was the hallmark of the human, not the machine.

In order to identify the human, the judge's method must be based on tasks that humans can easily handle and that computers stumble upon. One of those aspects is humour - like for example, in this short joke: "Have you heard of the new restaurant called Karma? It has no menu, you get what you deserve": the judge tells the funny story and asks A and B to explain where and why you should laugh. Another aspect is the news, a set of points that everyone is informed about and that can be used as a basis

---

[4] Elamrani et Yampolskiy suggest that all the tests implies one human who interprets the interaction and favors an approach that is either oriented to the architecture, or to the behaviour.

for an identification attempt. One can also engage a computer in a conversation that deals with all kinds of subjects (for example, science, history, art, entertainment, music, etc.), which represents a high level of difficulty. Turing's idea seems correct in principle, because if you can fool a judge with a program, then your computer is operating in a mode that resembles intelligence. The fact remains that, even with the best programs, the result is still often only a simulated conversation that does not deceive a human judge for a long time.

3.2 Limits of the Intelligence Tests

Some philosophers, among them Searle, believe that even if you manage to complete a program that passes the Turing test, it does not prove that you have put intelligence into the computer [17]. This is his famous thought experiment of the Chinese Room in which an individual who does not speak a word of Chinese can nevertheless use a set of language rules and thus apply them to have a conversation in Chinese. Searle states that the non-Chinese speaker can provide correct answers from a syntactic point of view, when he or she understands nothing about the meaning of the symbols he or she manipulates from a semantic point of view. This is meant to show that computer programs are syntactic, they are only tools to manipulate symbols, while human thoughts have a semantic content, a meaning which is attached to words. The meaning of words in language is not reduced to syntax, because it comes from biophysical properties of our neurons that a program cannot possess. Hence this basic idea that programs cannot think: literally speaking, a computer does not speak Chinese, for it does not understand this language as humans can do... The machines will therefore never be intelligent, even if they pass the Turing Test, because the latter is not a sufficient condition for the intelligence of a machine[5].

Another criticism of the Turing test was made by French, who argued that passing the test is not a necessary condition of intelligence [18]. He imagines the story of a people who would know only one species of bird, the seagull, and would face the problem of making a flying machine. In order to determine if they are successful in this project, these people would use the seagull test in which a machine is flying if it cannot be distinguished from a seagull whose behaviour is observed with help of a radar. The radar limits the precision of the request for imitation as the dialogue, by means of typed exchanges, limits the precision of the request for imitation in the implementation of the Turing test. In this test, planes, helicopters, hot air balloons and even other birds will not pass the seagull test and will therefore not be considered able of fly. Thus, the Turing test is perhaps a sufficient condition of intelligence, but of human intelligence, and it is linked to the language used for dialogues, which prevents it from being considered universal. It may well also be that many of our behaviours are highly dependent on the particular way in which our brain processes information at the deepest level, the one which of the subcognitive processes [18].

---

[5] Now, Searle might admit that if one day the machines succeed in faithfully imitating humans, we would no doubt have to change our position, against a vision that by principle seems to reserve intelligence to humans.

3.3   Tests for the Sentience of a Machine

One can also imagine a test of humanity for the sentience of a machine in order to assess its ability to "feel" like a human in the interaction it can have with him or her. It is not certain that this kind of test should be based on that of Turing, but it can be fruitful to explore this track, as already envisaged by Campbell who speaks of a game of human imitation (*Imitation Man*) [19]. Attention is focused on the conversation between a judge J, a human H and a machine M, but the main difference in the sentience test is that the content of information and the mode of communication are not the only things that counts. It is also information and communication as it shows a set of aspects of a partner's behaviour that testify the presence of a sentience in the language itself. It is therefore a linguistic evidence which grounds the Judge J's judgment in the absence of access by the judge to physical data which could express the psychic state of A and B.

The test of humanity of a machine is moved towards the expression of sentience in verbal language, towards what reveals the sensation, the emotion, the sentiment or even the consciousness of A or B. This expression of sentience in language supposes not only an information content, but also a mode of communication. Now, if we stick to a classic Turing test, this implies that it can only be a verbal communication, to the exclusion of any non-verbal one which would pass through expressions of the body (gestures, facial expressions, etc.). It is therefore in the realm of the language used by the speaker that the sentience can reside, as when A or B says: "I have a toothache, it's been a long time since it happened to me. It's a pain that takes me to the bottom molar, on the right side, and goes down into the gums." Or when A or B answers, to a question asked about its isolation and its awareness of it: "Yes, I feel a little lonely in this room, and I must say that, usually, I am rather someone who likes the presence of others." If a machine M is able to express itself in this way, a judge J can conclude that it is a human H who communicates this message to him or her.

Now, one could also conceive that the sentience test takes into account, according to the access clause to physical information, and consequently, to psychic information, the non-verbal communication. The information and the communication of a machine M should then not only be taken for that of a human H by a judge J, but it should be also by virtue of a certain behaviour of the body. This supposes that, in its dynamic aspect, that of non-verbal communication, if however it is coherently coupled to verbal communication, a machine is identical to a human. It would be so if a machine M, of strictly human aspect, begins to get angry, with the blood rising to the cheeks, the sound of the voice raising, the arms waggling, while saying to children: "Listen, I have told you several times not to touch this Ming vase. Are you an idiot?" Now, we are entitled to wonder if verbal and non-verbal communication and the coherent coupling between the two do not requires something like a "grammar" of expressions. It is certainly this common grammar that judge J should share with machine M and human H in order to produce a correct interpretation of their behaviour.

3.4 Limits of the Sentience Tests

Searle is also famous for developing the pragmatics, the study of speech acts which supposes that the meaning of a statement depends on the speaker intentions and on the speech situation [20]. The speech act can succeed or fail depending on the situation, like when I say "I baptise this ship Queen Mary" and the conditions for success are or are not satisfied. For instance, I am achieving this baptism with a bottle of champagne, but the bottle does not break on the hull, which is interpreted as a failure of the speech act, since the ship is not properly baptised. Behind the intention of a speech act stands the intentionality, the relation of consciousness to an object, which can be extended by considering the background of this relation, the tendency or the disposition of belief and desire [21]. This notion of intentionality can be useful beyond intelligence for the sentience test as a necessary condition in order to give a meaning to an action. Now, one could argue that it is not a sufficient condition, in the sense that, if a machine passed the sentience test, it would not prove that it has intentionality. It would just prove that it behaves in action and communication as if it had an intentionality, but without experiencing sensation or emotion, neither desire and belief. In this respect, no more than syntax, the pragmatics of action would allow access to the meaning of words, if these depend on intentionality and are empty of any intention, desire or belief.

A more radical objection puts forward the idea of the "philosophical zombie", as in Kirk's thought experiment, according to which it is possible that a being has all the characteristics of a human, but is found lacking in sentience [22]. One can imagine as a logical possibility that an organism or even a machine cannot be distinguished from a normal human being, in its bodily and behavioural aspects, but that he feels nothing[6]. Thus, the being in question could for example be struck by an object, but not feel any pain, while giving the appearance in his reaction that he did feel pain. The argument is quite close in the spirit to that of the doctrine of physicalism and amounts to saying that consciousness is nothing more than a physical phenomenon. However, some researchers in artificial intelligence, like Minsky, try to show that the argument is circular: the possibility of something physically identical to a human, but deprived of subjective experience, assumes that the physical characters of humans are not what produce experience... which is contradictory to physicalism. It follows as far as artificial sentience is concerned that the relation between the physical aspects of the bodily behaviour is also narrowly coupled with the psychic activity of a mind endowed with a subjective experience - the "hard problem" of consciousness for Chalmers [13].

4 Human-Machine Interaction

A significant number of humanity tests give primacy to the interaction between the human and the machine, on the narrow mode if the interaction is bounded to conversation, on a broader mode if it includes the behaviour in action. This is all the

---

[6] As stated by Kirk, «it is at least logically possible for there to be an organism indistinguishable from a normal human being in all anatomical, behavioral and other respects, yet insentient», p. 43.

difference between a partial Turing test (*Turing 1*) and a total Turing test (*Turing 2*), but one can wonder if the first kind, with its restrictive clause of conversation, is still relevant.

If it is considered obsolete, the move to the second kind of test, which widens it to action and behaviour, results in the production of machines that in their physical aspect can be confused with humans. This clause also assumes that the behaviour of these machines is like a door open on a psychic life which must have a certain form, or structure, and show some coherence. But perhaps this is too demanding a clause, for it suggests that humans themselves would be fully coherent beings, while simple ordinary experience proves the opposite. It is therefore towards the idea of a *personality* of machines, endowed with a certain character, coupled with a certain temper, that it would be wise to direct the reflection on the action of artificial devices. But the personality of a machine, if such a thing exists, cannot be kept aside from the codes of a society or a culture which owns a certain "grammar" of the person and for some of them only refers to the notion of *Ego*.

All in all, the Humaniter as an idea is a machine which not only *thinks* like a human, *feels* like a human, but also can coordinate these two kinds of abilities and link them to another one, action, so that the machine also *acts* like a human. One could thus suggest that the idea of a Humaniter, as a total machine, requires not only the principle of AI, the principle of AS, but also the principle of AA: Artificial Action. This AA Principle could be formulated as follows: *A machine can act like a human*. Thus, a Humaniter is a machine which articulates the functions and abilities of the Reasoner, the Cogniter, the Voliter, the Experiencer and, finally, the Actor. This is a point to keep in mind in the project of making a both intelligent and sentient machine, namely a machine that properly speaking is not and cannot be a Humaniter, but that nevertheless can be a machine with a human face.

References

1. Gâcogne, L.: Intelligence Artificielle. Ellipses, Paris (2015)
2. Julia, L.: L'intelligence artificielle n'existe pas. 1st Edn., Edi8, Paris, France (2019)
3. Matson, W.I.: Sentience. University of California Press, Berkeley, Los Angeles (1982)
4. Husain, A.: The Sentient Machine. Scribner, New York (2017)
5. Breton, P.: A l'image de l'homme Du Golem aux créatures virtuelles. Seuil, Paris (1995)
6. Kurzweil, R.: The Singularity is Near: How Humans Transcend Biology. Viking Penguin Group, New York (2005)
7. Descartes, R.: Méditations Métaphysiques. Vrin, Paris (2019)
8. Wittgenstein, L.: Remarks on the Philosophy of Psychology, 3rd edn. Wiley Blackwell, Malden, Oxford (1998)
9. Gardner, H.: Frames of Mind: The Theory of Multiple Intelligence. Basic Books, New York (1983)
10. Wittgenstein, L.: Philosophical Investigations, 4th edn. Wiley Blackwell, Malden, Oxford (2009)
11. Perkins, M.: Sensing the World. Hackett Publishing, Indianapolis (1983)
12. Scarantino, A.: Emotion. Stanford Encyclopedia of Philosophy (2018)
13. Chalmers, D.J.: The Character of Consciousness. Oxford University Press, Oxford (2010)

14. Elamrani, A., Yampolskiy, R.: Reviewing tests for machine consciousness. J. Conscious. Stud. **26**(5–6), 35–64 (2019)
15. Harnard, S.: Can machine be conscious? How? J. Conscious. Stud. **10**(4–5), 67–75 (2003)
16. Turing, A.: Computing machinery and intelligence. Mind **49**, 433–460 (1950)
17. Searle, J.: Minds, brains and programs. Behav. Brain Sci. **3**(3), 417–457 (1980)
18. French, R.M.: Subcognition and the limits of the turing test. Mind **99**, 53–65 (1990)
19. Campbell, K.: Body and Mind. University of Notre-Dame Press, Notre Dame (1984)
20. Searle, J.: Speech Acts. Cambridge University Press, Cambridge (1969)
21. Searle, J.: Intentionality. Cambridge University Press, Cambridge (1988)
22. Kirk, R.: Sentience and behaviour. Mind **83**(329), 43–60 (1974)

Medical Dialogue Summarization for Automated Reporting in Healthcare

Sabine Molenaar[✉], Lientje Maas, Verónica Burriel, Fabiano Dalpiaz,
and Sjaak Brinkkemper

Department of Information and Computing Sciences,
Utrecht University, Utrecht, The Netherlands
{s.molenaar,j.a.m.maas,v.burriel,f.dalpiaz,s.brinkkemper}@uu.nl

Abstract. Healthcare providers generally spend excessive time on administrative tasks at the expense of direct patient care. The emergence of new artificial intelligence and natural language processing technologies gives rise to innovations that could relieve them of this burden. In this paper, we present a pipeline structure for building dialogue summarization systems. Our pipeline summarizes a consultation of a patient with a care provider and automatically generates a report compliant with medical formats. Four pipeline components are used to generate a report based on audio input. The outputs of each component are analyzed to determine the most important challenges and issues. The current proof-of-concept, which was applied to eight doctor-to-patient sessions concerning ear infection, shows that automatic dialogue summarization and reporting is achievable, but requires improvements to increase completeness.

Keywords: Dialogue summarization · Automated reporting · Natural language processing · Artificial intelligence · Healthcare

1 Introduction

The introduction of the Electronic Medical Record (EMR) was intended to improve the communication among care providers within and between healthcare institutions. The EMR contains information about patients such as medical history, vital signs and medication among others. In addition, the EMR demands guideline adherence and may, in some uses, provide decision support [7].

While the EMR aims to improve patient care, this may not always be the case. Administrative burden in healthcare is a well-known problem, especially in general practice, psychiatric care, and trauma surgery [12,28]. In the US, a first year resident spends more time with the EMR than with patients [8].

As a solution to these problems, the Care2Report project strives for automated reporting in healthcare [18]. The goal is to automatically generate medical reports of patient-doctor dialogues in compliance with clinical guidelines and

S. Dupuy-Chessa and H. A. Proper (Eds.): CAiSE 2020 Workshops, LNBIP 382, pp. 76–88, 2020.
https://doi.org/10.1007/978-3-030-49165-9_7

without disrupting the current way of working. This is the research framework within which we position this paper.

Starting from the vision and overall architecture of Care2Report [18], we focus here on a detailed study of the dialogue summarization pipeline, which aims to support speech and text processing in healthcare by combining computational linguistics and AI techniques. After a brief description of the pipeline structure, we investigate difference facets of *quality*. We make the following contributions:

1. We study how quality in the pipeline can be measured and which threats can affect quality;
2. We evaluate the quality of the pipeline and its components by analyzing eight reports generated by the proof-of-concept;
3. We identify which threats have affected the quality to provide a basis for further improvement of the pipeline.

The paper is structured as follows. Sect. 2 describes related work. We present the dialogue summarization pipeline in Sect. 3. We describe metrics of and threats to quality in Sect. 4. We report on an analysis of eight medical consultations in Sect. 5. Finally, we present limitations and outline future work in Sect. 6.

2   Related Works

An extensive study on the effect of the EMR on doctor-patient communication [2] revealed several benefits, such as improved understanding by the patient and a positive communication experience with the EMR. However, several concerns were identified, both from the perspective of patients and doctors. In case of the former, patients expressed worries about the doctor potentially getting distracted by the computer during the appointment. The latter mentioned not being able to tend to the patient while interacting with the computer at the same time. In addition, it is reported that doctors spent an estimated 32% of the appointment interacting with the computer (based on an average of six studies). In three studies, patients were found to stop talking whenever the doctor was typing [2]. Another issue is the potential loss of emotional and/or psychosocial elements. Non-verbal communication (e.g., eye contact) is important for sharing emotions between patient and physician and such information may be overlooked if the physician is interacting with the EMR [22]. In summary, challenges arise when medical staff needs to interact with the EMR during direct patient care.

In the healthcare domain, various attempts have been made to automatically generate documents concerned with patient data. Firstly, speech recognition is a prominent approach to reducing time spent on reporting in healthcare, as studies frequently make use of dictating after a consultation [1]. In the Netherlands, however, a mere 1% of medical staff makes use of speech recognition. Reasons for the lack of adoption are, reportedly, interference with doctors' normal way of working, lack of support by hospitals and financial limitations [17]. Secondly,

Klann & Szolovits delivered a proof-of-concept framework that captures the dialogue during a doctor-patient meeting. Their approach covers the entire dialogue, rather than a report of the consultation [14]. More recently, Chiu *et al.* developed and tested a system that transcribes conversations between doctors and patients. Their best model resulted in a word error rate of 18.3% [9]. Again, this system delivers a medical transcription, rather than an EMR update or a report. Finally, the BabyTalk project utilizes a prototype that generates summaries in text, using physiological signals and events performed by medical staff as input. While the prototype proved to be able to generate proper summaries of clinical data, the texts provided by human experts were still superior [21].

Jiang *et al.* [13] discuss the use of AI in healthcare and conclude that both linguistics (through NLP) and AI (via Machine Learning, ML) are used to enrich medical data. In their study, NLP uses human language notes as input and returns a structured version of these notes for the EMR. Then, the EMR data feeds ML algorithms. The summarization pipeline aims to combine the two rather than execute them sequentially: both NLP and ML are used to enrich the data stored in the EMR. Without taking precautions, neural networks may overlook rare outcomes, due to the under-representation of these outcomes in training data [26]. Another possible disadvantage of using (deep) neural networks is that they often lack transparency, which limits their use in the healthcare domain [15].

3   Dialogue Summarization Pipeline

We use the term *dialogue summarization pipeline* to refer to the set of software components required to generate reports using audio input [18]. We define a pipeline as a series of (NLP- and/or AI-enabled) computational components, which transform output from one system into input for another system.

The pipeline combines AI and computational linguistics algorithms to automatically generate reports through the components shown in Fig. 1. Example outputs generated by the components using real-world input (from patient-General Practitioner (GP) consultations) are depicted in boxes with dashed arrows (note that the original audio input was in Dutch and was translated for the purpose of this example). First, a **speech transcription** is made using the audio of the dialogue as input. Subsequently, the **triple extraction** component extracts semantic triples from the transcription. Semantic triples consist of subjects, predicates and objects respectively [4]. A domain-specific example of a triple is: $\langle Ear, hasSymptom, Pain \rangle$. In a separate component, triples are utilized for **ontology population**. The ontology contains domain-specific information, such as clinical guidelines and standards. Once the ontology contains the guidelines for a specific illness, it does not need to be populated for this illness again. Ideally, the ontology will contain all the clinical guidelines and will only be modified if changes to the original guidelines are made.

Thirdly, triples are selected in the **triple matching** component. Extracted triples are selected if they match triples in the ontology. For instance, in Fig. 1, one of the triples is $\langle Patient, has, Earache \rangle$, which can be matched to part of

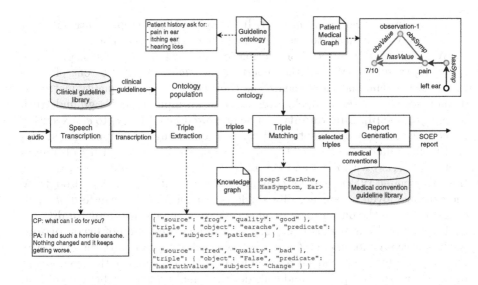

Fig. 1. Dialogue summarization pipeline for reporting in healthcare.

the guidelines shown at the top *"Patient history ask for: pain in ear"*. All the triples that are matched in this manner are selected to be included in the report and are stored in a graph. This graph contains an overview of the patient's symptoms, the findings by the GP, the diagnosis and the treatment.

To avoid affecting the way of working of care providers, the report is generated in compliance with medical conventions. For example, GPs in the Netherlands use the SOEP (or SOAP) format, which defines four sections for reporting on a consultation: Subjective (S), Objective (O), Evaluation (E) (or Assessment (A)) and Plan (P) [6]. When the triples are matched, they are also categorized, to ensure they are included in the correct place in the format or report. Finally, the categorized triples are transformed back into natural language by the **report generation** component, to make them easier to read and understand.

4 Quality in the Dialogue Summarization Pipeline

We first describe the quality metrics that can be used for assessing the performance of individual components of a pipeline or of the pipeline as a whole in Sect. 4.1. Then, we discuss how to cope with threats that affect the performance of the dialogue summarization pipeline in Sect. 4.2.

4.1 Measuring Quality in a Pipeline

A pipeline consists of multiple components that are sequentially connected: $(c_1, \ldots, c_n)$. Since each component is an imperfect data processor, the outcomes of that component will contain error. Intuitively, at each step, additional error is potentially introduced, thereby affecting the quality of the pipeline.

We define quality in terms of information retrieval metrics such as precision, recall, F_β-score, etc. We use the generic term *quality* to refer to one of these metrics, or a combination of them. The choice of the specific quality metrics is domain specific. Given a pipeline $(c_1, \ldots, c_n)$, an input i_1 and a ground truth output gt_n, the **pipeline quality** can be measured by feeding i_1 to c_1, executing in sequence all the components until c_n, and comparing the output against gt_n.

Pipeline quality can be used to assess the quality of a sub-sequence of components $(c_i, \ldots, c_k)$ with $i \geq 1$ and $k \leq n$, by feeding gt_{i-1} as input to c_i, running the sub-pipeline till c_k, and by comparing the output against gt_k. Brought to the extreme, given a sequence of a single component (c_i), we can feed gt_{i-1} to c_i and compare the output against gt_i to measure the **component quality**.

Inspired by Valls-Vargas *et al.* [27], we consider the notion of **error propagation**: given a sub-pipeline $(c_i, \ldots, c_k)$, we feed gt_{i-1} to c_i and run the entire pipeline to obtain some output o', then feed gt_{k-1} to c_k and run that component to obtain another output o'', and consider the quality difference between o'' and o'. Such a difference denotes how much error in c_k is introduced by c_i.

The measures of pipeline quality, component quality and error propagation provide a comprehensive picture of how a pipeline performs, also how the earlier components of a pipeline affect the performance of a later component.

4.2 Handling with Quality Threats

Table 1 lists the major threats that affect the quality of a pipeline's processing. The list is not meant to be exhaustive, but it rather serves as a summary of the challenges to consider in order to maximize quality.

The **speech transcription** component suffers from well known challenges in automated speech recognition [10]. For example, background noise makes it harder for the algorithms to distinguish the voices of the participants in the conversation. Moreover, when multiple voices participate in the conversation, they have to be distinguished [25]. Out-of-vocabulary words pose a challenge, as the algorithm is unable to match the recorded sound to a word within its prior knowledge. Finally, in the context of dialogue summarization, it is reasonable to expect that the people in the conversation may have accents or employ dialect.

Regarding **triple extraction**, the existing challenges arise from computational linguistics. A common problem refers to non-trivial sentence fragments such as compound nouns and phrasal verbs. For example, a phrasal verb such as 'to search for' it not easy to map to a triple; take the sentence 'I was searching my cupboard for my pills' could result either in a triple $\langle I, search, Cupboard \rangle$ or in a triple $\langle I, searchFor, Pills \rangle$. Furthermore, coreference resolution is a well-known issue [19], which refers to how pronouns can be linked to the noun they refer to. The use of pronouns such as 'it' or 'which' are common in medical consultations. Conflicting statements are also a hard to tackle; consider the following dialogue: (i) [patient] 'my hand hurts'; (ii) [doctor] 'you are indicating your finger, so I

Table 1. Overview of the quality threats within the dialogue summarization pipeline.

Component	Threat to quality
Speech transcription	T1: Background noise
	T2: Multiple voices in the conversation
	T3: Out-of-vocabulary words
	T4: Accent, dialect, and spontaneous speech
Triple extraction	T5: Compound nouns and phrasal verbs
	T6: Coreference resolution
	T7: Conflicting statements
Triple matching	T8: Incompleteness of ontology
	T9: Omission of relevant information out of context
	T10: Different categorization of measuring values
	T11: Redundancy of information (synonyms detection)
Report generation	T12: Erroneous triple categorization (SOEP)
	T13: Wrong positioning of information in text

suppose your finger hurts' – in this case, only the doctor's statement should be considered for triplification, but it is hard to reliably do so.

The quality of **triple matching** could also be affected by several threats. One of them is the incompleteness of the ontology. The building and population of the ontology is a component described in [18] that only needs to be done during the development phase of the system and could involve some threats to the triple matching component. If this ontology is incomplete or has been populated for a very specific medical specialization, some concepts could be missing, and therefore the triple matching process could discard relevant information. Also, some relevant information to be included in the final report could be discarded if it belongs to a non-medical domain and it is not included in the ontology or it is not mentioned in the clinical guidelines. For instance, some experience lived by the patient, which could look like an anecdote to omit in the report, but maybe it is the precursor of the disease. Another threat to be taken into account is the way of measuring some values. For example, pain can be measured from 1 to 10, or from soft to strong, or from light to hard, etc. Despite these different categories, *1, soft* and *light* are representing the same level of pain and this could cause errors in the categorization if this is not taken into account during the matching process. Also, some information can be repeated by the care provider or the patient, even using synonyms. This redundancy should be detected while doing the matching to avoid redundancy in the generated report.

During **report generation**, some challenges arise to ensure the quality of the final report. One important part of this component is the categorization of the triples according to the SOEP convention. If a triple is categorized in a wrong section, not only the information of this triple is missing in the corresponding section, but the correctness of the wrongly assigned section is also affected. Once this categorization is done, the Natural Language Generation process starts. During this process, the relevant triples are ordered (text planning), each triple is converted into a standalone sentence (lexicalization) and some of these sentences are merged into longer ones (aggregation) [18]. Assuring a correct order of the triples in the text planning and aggregation phases is essential to avoid incorrect meanings and interpretations of the information collected during the consultation, which could cause erroneous statements in the final report.

5   Analysis of Automatically Generated Reports

We build a proof-of-concept implementation of our pipeline. In the current implementation, we rely on Google Speech for the speech-to-text transcription. For the triple extraction component, three different triple analyzers are used: Frog [5], FRED [11], Ollie [23]. The former supports Dutch, while the other two only support English, for these the transcriptions are translated from Dutch to English using Google Translate. The ontology was populated using clinical standards[1] that GPs in the Netherlands use to examine and diagnose patients. Matched triples are stored in a custom component, the patient medical graph [18]. Triples are transformed into natural language sentences using an extension of NaturalOWL [3] that supports the Dutch language.

The pipeline was tested on eight real-world consultations concerning external and middle ear infection. Transcriptions of the consultations were provided as input for the system, resulting in automatically generated medical reports, according to the SOEP convention. On average, the reports consisted of 1,132 words, ranging between 568 words (R-4) and 1,767 words (R-6).

We assessed the quality of the reports and of the intermediate results of the components in the pipeline (Fig. 1). Four out of five results of components in the pipeline are analyzed: transcription, triples, selected triples, and the SOEP report. If items are missing in the generated reports, we attempt to determine where these 'went missing' by tracing backward through the intermediate results.

Golden Standard. The SOEP format does not include any metrics with which to measure report quality and completeness. In addition, to the best of our knowledge, medical professionals in the Netherlands do not receive any formal training on how to write such formatted reports. Therefore, in order to determine the quality of the generated reports, we will rely on consultation reports, written by a GP in the SOEP format, which we use as a golden standard [16].

5.1   Report Quality

The eight generated reports were compared to the golden standard. We measure pipeline quality using three metrics: precision, recall and false positives (FPs). The quality of the reports was assessed according to the following process. Firstly, the number of items included in the generated and golden standards

---

[1] https://www.nhg.org/nhg-standaarden.

was established. Since GPs do not always include full sentences, but also partial phrases or even just words, the term 'item' needs to be defined. In this case, an item can be defined as a word or a sequence of words. Items are separated from each other using conjunctions (e.g., "and") and/or punctuation (e.g., periods, commas). Secondly, precision and recall were calculated. Thirdly, the number of false positives was determined, by counting items that were included in the generated report and items that are incorrectly included (i.e., partial items). An example of the latter is when the generated Plan includes *"paracetamol"*, while the golden standard explicitly states *"no paracetamol"*.

The number of items included for each section of the SOEP format by the generated (R-x) and golden standard (S-x) of the consultations (C-x) are shown in Table 2. For the generated reports the number of true positives (TPs), FPs and false negatives (FNs) are also shown, respectively.

Table 2. Number of items included for each section of the SOEP format, with TPs/FPs/FNs for the generated reports.

	C-1		C-2		C-3		C-4		C-5		C-6		C-7		C-8	
	R-1	S-1	R-2	S-2	R-3	S-3	R-4	S-4	R-5	S-5	R-6	S-6	R-7	S-7	R-8	S-8
S	1/0/3	4	1/0/8	9	1/0/4	5	0/0/4	4	0/0/4	4	0/0/9	9	0/0/8	8	0/0/8	8
O	0/0/2	2	0/1/6	6	2/0/1	3	1/1/8	9	0/0/4	4	0/0/4	4	1/0/2	3	1/0/1	2
E	0/0/1	1	0/0/2	2	1/0/0	1	1/0/1	2	0/0/2	2	0/0/1	1	0/0/1	1	0/0/1	1
P	0/2/1	1	3/1/5	8	1/1/1	2	1/0/2	3	1/0/5	6	0/2/5	5	0/1/2	2	2/0/0	2

It is apparent that the golden standards tend to consist of more items than the generated reports. The precision, recall, F1-score and number of FPs of each of the generated reports are presented in Table 3.

Table 3. Analysis of relevance and completeness of generated reports using the precision, recall and F-measure.

	R-1	R-2	R-3	R-4	R-5	R-6	R-7	R-8	μ
Precision	0.333	0.667	0.833	0.750	1.000	0.000	0.500	1.000	0.635
Recall	0.125	0.160	0.455	0.167	0.063	0.000	0.071	0.231	0.159
F1-score	0.182	0.258	0.588	0.273	0.112	0.000	0.125	0.375	0.239
FPs	2	2	1	1	0	2	1	0	1.125

Since we consider relevance (precision) and completeness (recall) to be equally important, the F1-score is calculated by assigning equal weight to both. Six out of eight reports achieved a precision score of half or higher, with the average being 0.635, meaning that the majority of the selected items are relevant. The recall score, however, is much lower. On average, 15.9% of the items that are considered relevant are included, meaning that the majority of relevant items is missing. The Subjective section lacks most items, even though this section often includes a high frequency of items when written by a GP. The reason may be T9, i.e., the omission of out-of-context information (see Sect. 4).

Finally, nearly all reports include FPs. While some of these items are harmless, for example if they provide additional information that is not required, others can lead to inaccurate reporting. In *R-2*, *"antibiotics"* was included as an item, while the golden standard explicitly stated *"in consultation with patient no antibiotics"*. **Challenge 1:** The system should be able to recognize negations, in order to provide correct information.

5.2   Pipeline Analysis

We analyze the quality of the outputs of two automated components in the pipeline: triple extraction and triple matching. We omit the transcription component because, in our case, this activity was done manually. We also use the intermediate results to locate where the missing item in the report were lost.

Triple Extraction. Triples are extracted from text using three triple analyzers: FRED (78.3% of extracted triples), Ollie (15.3%) and Frog (6.5%). All extracted triples are checked for their quality and labeled as **good** or **bad** (see Fig. 1). If a triple contains an item of excessive length (e.g., a full sentence instead of one or a few words) and/or does not contain a reference to either the doctor or patient, the triple is given the label **bad**. Only between 0.9% and 2.1% of the triples are labeled **good** (on average 21.1 triples out of 1,367 based on eight reports).

Triple Matching. All matched triples end up in the generated report, however, not all matched triples receive the correct categorization according to the SOEP format (see T12 in Sect. 4). The only erroneous categorization is within the Plan section. Medication mentioned during the consultation is always assigned to the Plan, while sometimes it is part of the Subjective. This part is in essence 'the patient's side of the story' and may also include previously used medication. **Challenge 2:** The location of the item in the transcription can help mitigate these errors, by separating the Subjective and the Plan. In addition, the tense of verbs can be used, since they distinguish past medications from future ones.

Locating Missing Report Items. When compared to the golden standards, the generated reports lacked 106 items. To determine at which point in the pipeline these items were lost (excluded or not identified), each missing item was traced back from the report to the transcript. Out of 106 items, only eleven could not be found in any of the intermediate results in the pipeline, as shown in Table 4. Note that the table does not show how many items were found, but the number of items that are still not identified in the particular output of the pipeline. Percentages are shown as portion of the total number of missing items.

All items that we found in the extracted triples (and yet were not included) had low quality. The analysis controller assesses the quality of the triples and distinguishes **good** and **bad** triples. 50.9% of the missing items were found in

Table 4. Overview of which missing items could not be located in the pipeline.

	R-1	R-2	R-3	R-4	R-5	R-6	R-7	R-8	%	μ
Missing items (total)	7	21	6	15	15	19	13	10	100.0%	13.3
In extracted triples	4	7	2	6	11	9	8	5	49.1%	6.5
In transcription (explicit)	0	3	1	2	4	4	1	0	14.2%	1.9
In transcription (fully)	1	0	0	3	3	2	2	0	10.4%	1.4

the extracted triples, but were all of bad quality. **Challenge 3:** Increasing the number of relevant items requires improving the quality of the triples.

A small portion of the items (14.2%) could only be located implicitly: they can be inferred from the transcript, but are not explicitly mentioned. An example of an implicit item is an explanation or recommendation given by the care provider to the patient. The GP does not announce that they will explain something, but this can be observed when reading the text. Another example is that the GP may state they will perform some medical action on the patient tomorrow, which means that the patient will return for another appointment, but this second appointment is not made explicit. **Challenge 4:** Conversation analysis techniques can be utilized to extract implicit information from transcripts.

The items that could not be located in any of the intermediate results in the pipeline are either observations or decisions made by the GP or gestures. Examples of observations are: (1) whether the eardrum is visible; this is part of the clinical guideline for ear infection, but the doctor makes no utterance about it, (2) if the ear canal is red, which only sometimes is mentioned out loud. Decisions made by the GP mostly refer to the diagnosis and plan. Based on the observations, they conclude a diagnosis which may or may not be communicated to the patient explicitly. Furthermore, the plan is discussed with the patient, but not in full detail. For instance, the GP will explain the patient receives ear drops, but does not specify how many of these drops they should use per day, while this is included in the report. The system, however, does allow the GP to add, modify or remove text in the report if necessary. Finally, it is hard to ascribe gestures to the GP or the patient (see T6 in Sect. 4). Oftentimes, patient mention *"I don't hear anything on this side"* or *"do you want to see the other ear as well"*, in combination with pointing the GP is able to tell which ear they are referring to, but based on text alone the system cannot distinguish between left and right. **Challenge 5:** Video input can be used to enhance text that includes a gesture by disambiguating the antecedent to reference pronouns such as "this".

6   Discussion and Future Work

In this paper, we introduced a dialogue summarization pipeline as a series of components that can generate a report of a conversation. The quality of the pipeline was evaluated through eight real medical consultations regarding ear infections. We compared the automatically generated reports, as well as the intermediate results, to the reports produced by a GP. While the evaluation demonstrates feasibility, it also points out several limitations and challenges.

Limitations. More consultations are needed for a more reliable assessment of the pipeline's quality. However, the list of challenges in Sect. 5 suggest clear improvement points. Furthermore, the golden standards were written by a single GP; since medical students/professionals do not receive any formal training on writing reports using the SOEP format, other care providers might write slightly different reports. Papineni *et al.* referred to these situations as 'stylistic variations' [20]. Finally, some items in the golden standards are not mentioned explicitly and, thus, may not end up in the output of the triple extraction. To ensure that implicitly discussed relevant information is also extracted by the system, conversation analysis techniques are needed. For instance, when the patient and GP agree on a course of action, this is not contained in one sentence and can only be inferred from the dialogue between both [24].

Future Directions. We plan on generating more reports to acquire more data and to measure the effects of error propagation in the pipeline, as discussed in Sect. 4. We will ask more care providers to write reports in SOEP formats in order to be able to randomly select stylistic variations of golden standards to compare the output to. We also intend to include support for additional diseases and ailments by including them in the ontology. The results from our evaluation (the low number of **good** triples), together previous findings showing that over half of the utterances in the speech transcript are not relevant for reporting [18], call for relevance selection algorithms that diminish the amount of unnecessary information that is stored. Furthermore, we intend to implement support for the two additional modalities, video and sensors, as well.

Conclusion. While the generated reports are still imperfect, the proof-of-concept shows that dialogue summarization using the proposed pipeline structure is achievable when sufficient engineering effort is put in optimizing the implementation. When sufficiently improved, our pipeline can help care providers reduce their administrative burden and focus on direct patient care.

References

1. Ajami, S.: Use of speech-to-text technology for documentation by healthcare providers. Nat. Med. J. India **29**(3), 148–152 (2016)
2. Alkureishi, M.A., et al.: Impact of electronic medical record use on the patient-doctor relationship and communication: a systematic review. J. Gen. Intern. Med. **31**(5), 548–560 (2016)
3. Androutsopoulos, I., Lampouras, G., Galanis, D.: Generating natural language descriptions from OWL ontologies: the NaturalOWL system. J. Artif. Intell. Res. **48**, 671–715 (2013)
4. Antoniou, G., Van Harmelen, F.: A Semantic Web Primer. MIT press, Cambridge (2004)
5. Bosch, A.V.D., Busser, B., Canisius, S., Daelemans, W.: An efficient memory-based morphosyntactic tagger and parser for Dutch. LOT Occas. Ser. **7**, 191–206 (2007)

6. Cameron, S., Turtle-Song, I.: Learning to write case notes using the SOAP format. J. Couns. Dev. **80**(3), 286–292 (2002)
7. Campanella, P., et al.: The impact of electronic health records on healthcare quality: a systematic review and meta-analysis. Eur. J. Public Health **26**(1), 60–64 (2015)
8. Chaiyachati, K.H., et al.: Assessment of inpatient time allocation among first-year internal medicine residents using time-motion observations. JAMA Intern. Med. **179**(6), 760–767 (2019)
9. Chiu, C.C., et al.: Speech recognition for medical conversations. arXiv preprint arXiv:1711.07274 (2017)
10. Deng, L., Huang, X.: Challenges in adopting speech recognition. Commun. ACM **47**(1), 69–75 (2004)
11. Gangemi, A., Presutti, V., Reforgiato Recupero, D., Nuzzolese, A.G., Draicchio, F., Mongiovì, M.: Semantic web machine reading with FRED. Seman. Web **8**(6), 873–893 (2017)
12. Golob Jr., J.F., Como, J.J., Claridge, J.A.: The painful truth: the documentation burden of a trauma surgeon. J. Trauma Acute Care Surg. **80**(5), 742–747 (2016)
13. Jiang, F., et al.: Artificial intelligence in healthcare: past, present and future. Stroke Vasc. Neurol. **2**(4), 230–243 (2017)
14. Klann, J.G., Szolovits, P.: An intelligent listening framework for capturing encounter notes from a doctor-patient dialog. BMC Med. Inform. Decis. Making **9**(1), S3 (2009)
15. Kollias, D., Tagaris, A., Stafylopatis, A., Kollias, S., Tagaris, G.: Deep neural architectures for prediction in healthcare. Complex Intell. Syst. **4**(2), 119–131 (2017). https://doi.org/10.1007/s40747-017-0064-6
16. Liu, C., Talaei-Khoei, A., Zowghi, D., Daniel, J.: Data completeness in healthcare: a literature survey. PAJAIS **9**(2), 75–100 (2017)
17. Luchies, E., Spruit, M., Askari, M.: Speech technology in Dutch health care: a qualitative study. In: HEALTHINF, pp. 339–348 (2018)
18. Maas, L., et al.: The Care2Report system: automated medical reporting as an integrated solution to reduce administrative burden in healthcare. In: Proceedings of HICSS (2020)
19. Ng, V.: Advanced machine learning models for coreference resolution. In: Poesio, M., Stuckardt, R., Versley, Y. (eds.) Anaphora Resolution. TANLP, pp. 283–313. Springer, Heidelberg (2016). https://doi.org/10.1007/978-3-662-47909-4_10
20. Papineni, K., Roukos, S., Ward, T., Zhu, W.J.: BLEU: a method for automatic evaluation of machine translation. In: Proceedings of ACL, pp. 311–318 (2002)
21. Portet, F., et al.: Automatic generation of textual summaries from neonatal intensive care data. Artif. Intell. **173**(7–8), 789–816 (2009)
22. Rathert, C., Mittler, J.N., Banerjee, S., McDaniel, J.: Patient-centered communication in the era of electronic health records: what does the evidence say? Patient Educ. Couns. **100**(1), 50–64 (2017)
23. Schmitz, M., Bart, R., Soderland, S., Etzioni, O., et al.: Open language learning for information extraction. In: Proceedings of EMNLP-CoNLL, pp. 523–534 (2012)
24. Sidnell, J., Stivers, T.: The Handbook of Conversation Analysis, vol. 121. Wiley, Hoboken (2012)
25. Snyder, D., Garcia-Romero, D., Sell, G., Povey, D., Khudanpur, S.: X-vectors: robust DNN embeddings for speaker recognition. In: Proceedings of ICASSP, pp. 5329–5333. IEEE (2018)

26. Syed, Z., Rubinfeld, I.: Unsupervised risk stratification in clinical datasets: identifying patients at risk of rare outcomes. In: Proceedings of ICML, pp. 1023–1030 (2010)
27. Valls-Vargas, J., Zhu, J., Ontanon, S.: Error analysis in an automated narrative information extraction pipeline. IEEE Trans. Comput. Intell. AI Games 9(4), 342–353 (2016)
28. Woolhandler, S., Himmelstein, D.U.: Administrative work consumes one-sixth of US physicians' working hours and lowers their career satisfaction. Int. J. Health Serv. 44(4), 635–642 (2014)

Towards the Integration of Agricultural Data from Heterogeneous Sources: Perspectives for the French Agricultural Context Using Semantic Technologies

Shufan Jiang[1,2](✉), Rafael Angarita[1], Raja Chiky[1], Stéphane Cormier[2], and Francis Rousseaux[2]

[1] Institut Supérieur d'Electronique de Paris, LISITE,
28 Rue Notre Dame des Champs, 75006 Paris, France
{shufan.jiang,rafael.angarita,raja.chiky}@isep.fr
[2] Université de Reims Champagne Ardenne, CReSTIC EA 3804,
CReSTIC - UFR Sciences Exactes et Naturelles - Moulin de la Housse - BP 1039,
51687 Reims CEDEX 2, France
{stephane.cormier,francis.rousseaux}@univ-reims.fr

Abstract. Sustainable agriculture is crucial to society since it aims at supporting the world's current food needs without compromising future generations. Recent developments in Smart Agriculture and Internet of Things have made possible the collection of unprecedented amounts of agricultural data with the goal of making agricultural processes better and more efficient, and thus supporting sustainable agriculture. These data coming from different types of IoT devices can also be combined with relevant information published in online social networks and on the Web in the form of textual documents. Our objective is to integrate such heterogeneous data into knowledge bases that can support farmers in their activities, and to present global, real-time and comprehensive information to researchers. Semantic technologies and linked data provide a possibility for data integration and for automatic information extraction. This paper aims to give a brief review on the current semantic web technology applications for agricultural corpus, then to discuss the limits and potentials in construction and maintenance of existing ontologies in agricultural domain.

Keywords: Ontology · Smart agriculture · Internet of Things (IoT) · Semantics · Data integration

1 Introduction

Recent advances in Information and Communication Technology (ICT) aim at tackling some of the most important challenges in agriculture we face today [5]. Supporting the world's current food needs without compromising future generations through sustainable agriculture is of great challenge. Indeed, among

© Springer Nature Switzerland AG 2020
S. Dupuy-Chessa and H. A. Proper (Eds.): CAiSE 2020 Workshops, LNBIP 382, pp. 89–94, 2020.
https://doi.org/10.1007/978-3-030-49165-9_8

all the topics around sustainable agriculture, how to reduce the usage, and the impact of pesticide without losing the quantity or quality in the yield to fulfill the requirement of the growing population has an increasingly important place [6].

Researchers have applied a wide range of technologies to tackle some specific goals. Among these goals: climate prediction in agriculture using simulation models [7], making the production of certain types of grains more efficient and effective with computer vision and Artificial Intelligence [11], soil assessment with drones [14], and the IoT paradigm when connected devices such as sensors capture real-time data at the field level and that, combined with Cloud Computing, can be used to monitor agricultural components such as soil, plants, animals and weather and other environmental conditions [16]. The usage of such ICTs to improve farming processes is known as *smart farming* [18].

In the context of smart farming, **IoT devices** themselves are both data producers and data consumers and they produce *highly-structured data*; however these devices and the technologies we presented above are far from being the only data sources. Indeed, important information related to agriculture can also come from different sources such as official periodic reports and journals like the French Plants Health Bulletins (BSV, for its name in French *Bulletin de Santé du Végétal*)[1], social media such as Twitter and farmers experiences. The goal of the BSV is to: i), present a report of crop health, including their stages of development, observations of pests and diseases, and the presence of symptoms related to them; and ii), provide an evaluation of the phytosanitary risk, according to the periods of crop sensitivity and the pest and disease thresholds. The BSV and other formal reports are *semi-structured data*.

In the agricultural context, **Twitter** -or any other social media- can be used as a platform for knowledge exchange about sustainable soil management [10] and it can also help the public to understand agricultural issues and support risk and crisis communication in agriculture [1]. **Farmer experiences** (aka Old farming practices or ancestral knowledge) may be collected through interviews and participatory processes. Social media posts and farmer experiences are *non-structured data*.

Figure 1 illustrates how this heterogeneous data coming from different sources may look like for farmers: information is not always explicit or timely. Our objective is to integrate such heterogeneous data into knowledge bases that can support farmers in their activities, and to present global, real-time and comprehensive information to researchers and interested parties. We present related work in Sect. 2, our initial approach in Sect. 3 and conclusions and perspectives in Sect. 4.

2   Previous Works

We classify existing works into two categories: information access and management in plant health domain, and data integration in agriculture. In the information access and management in plant health domain category, the *semantic annotation in BSV* focuses on extracting information for the traditional BSV.

---

[1] https://agriculture.gouv.fr/bulletins-de-sante-du-vegetal.

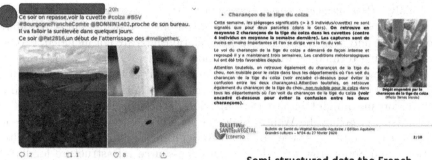

Fig. 1. Heterogeneous sources of agricultural data: *non-structured data* from Twitter and from farmers experiences www.bio-centre.org; *semi-structured data* from The French Plants Health Bulletins; and *structured data* from a weather sensor from www. data.gouv.fr.

Indeed, for more than 50 years, printed plant health bulletins have been diffused by regions and by crops in France, giving information about the arrival and the evolution of pests, pathogens, and weeds, and advises for preventive actions. These bulletins serve not only as agricultural alerts for farmers but also documentation for those who want to study the historical data. The French National Institute For Agricultural Research (INRA) has been working towards the publishing of the bulletins as Linked Open Data [12], where BSV from different regions are centralized, tagged with crop type, region, date and published on the Internet. To organize the bulletins by crop usage in France, an ontology with 272 concepts was manually constructed. With the volume of concepts and relations augmenting, manual construction of ontologies will become too expensive [3]. Thus, ontology learning methods to automatically extract concepts and relationships should be studied.

INRA has also introduced a method to modulate an ontology for crop observation [13]. The process is the following: 1) collect competency questions from researchers in agronomy; 2) construct the ontology corresponding to requirements in competency questions; 3) ask semantic experts who have not participated in the conception of the ontology to translate the competency questions into SPARQL queries to validate the ontology design. In this exercise, a model to describe the appearance of pests was given but not instantiated, nevertheless it could be a reference to our future crop-pest ontology conception.

Finally, *Pest observer* (http://www.pestobserver.eu/) is a web portal [15] which enables users to explore BSV with a combination of the following filters: crop, disease and pest; however, crop-pest relationships are not included. It relies on text-mining techniques to index BSV documents.

Regarding data integration in agriculture, $AGRIS^2$, the International System for Agricultural Science Technology states that many initiatives are developed to return more meaningful data to users [4]. Some of these initiatives are: extracting keywords by crawling the Web to build the AGROVOC vocabulary, which covers all areas of interest of the Food and Agriculture Organization of the United Nations; and SemaGrow [9], which is an open-source infrastructure for linked open data (LOD) integration that federates SPARQL endpoints from different providers. To extract pest and insecticide related relations, SemaGrow uses Computer-aided Ontology Development Architecture (CODA) for RDF triplification of Unstructured Information Management Architecture (UIMA) results from analysis of unstructured content.

Though INRA kick-started categorizing the french crop bulletins using linked open data, and that project SemaGrow shed light upon heterogeneous data integration using ontologies, both projects focused on processing formal and technical documents. Moreover, in CODA application case, IsPestOf rule was defined but not instantiated. Therefore, a global knowledge base, that covers the crops, the natural hazards including pests, diseases, and climate variations, and the relations between them, is still missing. There is also an increasing necessity to a comprehensive and an automatic approach to integrate knowledge from an ampler variety of heterogeneous sources.

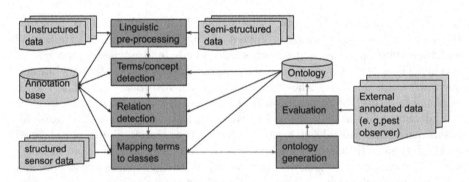

Fig. 2. Our approach for building a phytosanitary knowledge

3   Proposed Design

Figure 2 illustrates our initial design to manage the phytosanitary knowledge from heterogeneous data sources. It consists of a first phase based on ontology learning and a second phase based on ontology-based information extraction:

---

^{2} http://agris.fao.org.

- *Linguistic preprocessing*: Unstructured and semi-structured textual data are passed through a linguistic prepossessing pipeline (Sentence segmentation, Tokenization, Part-of-Speech (POS) tagging, Lemmatization) with existing natural language processing (NLP) tools such as Stanford NLP (https:// nlp.stanford.edu/), GATE (https://gate.ac.uk/) and UIMA (https://uima. apache.org/).
- *Terms/concept detection*: At the best of our knowledge and from the state of the art study, there is no ontology in french that modulates the natural hazards and their relations with crops. Existing french thesaurus like french crop usage and Agrovoc can be applied to filter collected data and served as gazetteer. Linguistic rules represented by regular expressions can be used to extract temporal data. Recurrent neural network (RNN), conditional random field (CRF) model and bidirectional long-short term memory (BiLSTM) were applied for health-related name entity recognition from twitter messages and gave a remarkable result [2]. Once the ontology is populated, it could provide knowledge and constraints to the extraction of terms [17].
- *Relation detection*: Similar to term/concept detection, initially there's no ontology. A basic strategy could be using self-supervised methods like Modified Open Information Extraction (MOIE): i) use wordnet-based semantic similarity and frequency distribution to identify related terms among detected terms from previous step ii) slicing the textual patterns between related terms [8]. Once the ontology is populated, it could contribute to calculate semantic similarities between detected terms in phase i).
- *Ontology generation*: Ontology generation with CODA and Pearl, as in the SemaGrow project presented in Sect. 2.
- *Evaluation*: This architecture presents a mutual application-based evaluation design: ideally the learned ontology should improve the information extraction. Besides, Pest observer web portal can be served to validate phytosanitary information extraction from plant health bulletins.

4   Conclusions and Perspectives

New digital technologies allow farmers to predict the yield of their fields, to optimize their resources and to avoid or protect their fields from natural hazards whether they are due to the weather, pests or diseases. This is a recent area where research is constantly evolving. We have introduced in this paper work relevant to our problem, namely: the integration of several data sources to extract information related to the natural hazards in agriculture. We then proposed an architecture based on ontology learning and ontology-based information extraction. We plan in a first phase build an ontology from twitter data that contains vocabulary in the existing thesaurus. To evaluate the constructed ontology, we will extract crops and pests from the learnt ontology, and compare it with tags in pest observer. In the following iterations, we will work on ontology alignment strategies to update the ontology with data from other sources. To go further, multilingual ontology management with keeping tempo-spacial contexts should be investigated.

References

1. Allen, K., Abrams, K., Meyers, C., Shultz, A.: A little birdie told me about agriculture: best practices and future uses of Twitter in agricultural communications. J. Appl. Commun. **94**(3), 6–21 (2010)
2. Batbaatar, E., Ryu, K.H.: Ontology-based healthcare named entity recognition from Twitter messages using a recurrent neural network approach. Int. J. Environ. Res. Public Health **19**, 3628 (2019)
3. Becka, H.W., Kima, S., Haganb, D.: A crop-pest ontology for extension publications. In: EFITA/WCCA Joint Congress on IT in Agriculture (2005)
4. Celli, F., Keizer, J., Jaques, Y., Konstantopoulos, S., Vudragović, D.: Discovering, indexing and interlinking information resources. F1000Research **4**, 432 (2015)
5. Cox, S.: Information technology: the global key to precision agriculture and sustainability. Comput. Electron. Agric. **36**(2–3), 93–111 (2002)
6. Ecophyto: Appel à projets - durabilité des systèmes de productions agricoles alternatifs (2019). Accessed 7 Mar 2020
7. Hammer, G., et al.: Advances in application of climate prediction in agriculture. Agric. Syst. **70**(2–3), 515–553 (2001)
8. Kaushik, N., Chatterjee, N.: Automatic relationship extraction from agricultural text for ontology construction. Inf. Process. Agric. **5**(1), 60–73 (2018)
9. Lokers, R., Konstantopoulos, S., Stellato, A., Knapen, M., Janssen, S.: Designing innovative linked open data and semantic technologies in agro-environmental modelling. In: 7th International Congress on Environmental Modelling and Software, Conference Date: 15–19 June 2014 (2014)
10. Mills, J., Reed, M., Skaalsveen, K., Ingram, J.: The use of Twitter for knowledge exchange on sustainable soil management. Soil Use Manag. **35**(1), 195–203 (2019)
11. Patrício, D.I., Rieder, R.: Computer vision and artificial intelligence in precision agriculture for grain crops: a systematic review. Comput. Electron. Agric. **153**, 69–81 (2018)
12. Roussey, C., et al.: A methodology for the publication of agricultural alert bulletins as LOD. Comput. Electron. Agric. **142**, 632–650 (2017)
13. Roussey, C., Ghorfi, T.A.: Annotation sémantique pour une interrogation experte des Bulletins de Santé du Végétal. In: Ranwez, S. (ed.) 29es Journées Francophones d'Ingénierie des Connaissances, IC 2018, AFIA, Nancy, France, pp. 37–52, July 2018
14. Tripicchio, P., Satler, M., Dabisias, G., Ruffaldi, E., Avizzano, C.A.: Towards smart farming and sustainable agriculture with drones. In: 2015 International Conference on Intelligent Environments, pp. 140–143. IEEE (2015)
15. Turenne, N., Andro, M., Corbière, R., Phan, T.T.: Open data platform for knowledge access in plant health domain: VESPA mining. CoRR abs/1504.06077 (2015)
16. Patil, V.C., Al-Gaadi, K.A., Biradar, D.P., Rangaswamy, M.: Internet of things (IoT) and cloud computing for agriculture: an overview (2012)
17. Wimalasuriya, D., Dou, D.: Ontology-based information extraction: an introduction and a survey of current approaches. J. Inf. Sci. **36**, 306–323 (2010)
18. Wolfert, S., Ge, L., Verdouw, C., Bogaardt, M.J.: Big data in smart farming-a review. Agric. Syst. **153**, 69–80 (2017)

Combination of Topic Modelling and Decision Tree Classification for Tourist Destination Marketing

Evripides Christodoulou[1], Andreas Gregoriades[1(✉)],
Maria Pampaka[2], and Herodotos Herodotou[1]

[1] Cyprus University of Technology, Limassol, Cyprus
ep.xristodoulou@edu.cut.ac.cy, {andreas.gregoriades,
herodotos.herodotou}@cut.ac.cy
[2] The University of Manchester, Manchester, UK
maria.pampaka@manchester.ac.uk

Abstract. This paper applies a smart tourism approach to tourist destination marketing campaigns through the analysis of tourists' reviews from TripAdvisor to identify significant patterns in the data. The proposed method combines topic modelling using Structured Topic Analysis with sentiment polarity, information on culture, and purchasing power of tourists for the development of a Decision Tree (DT) to predict tourists' experience. For data collection and analysis, several custom-made python scripts were used. Data underwent integration, cleansing, incomplete data processing, and imbalance data treatments prior to being analysed. The patterns that emerged from the DT are expressed in terms of rules that highlight variable combinations leading to negative or positive sentiment. The generated predictive model can be used by destination management to tailor marketing strategy by targeting tourists who are more likely to be satisfied at the destination according to their needs.

Keywords: Topic modelling · Sentiment analysis · Decision tree · Tourists' reviews

1 Introduction

With the recent information explosion as a result of the proliferation of data from social media, a new challenge emerged to discover information patterns hidden in big data using effective data mining techniques [19]. Micro-blogs are small messages communicated via social media such as Twitter, and gained popularity recently as means of expressing peoples' views [6]. Micro-blogs fall under the category of unstructured big data and are considered a type of electronic word of mouth (eWOM). A significant amount of eWOM are generated as part of consumers' evaluations of products and the hospitality services they are linked to [2, 33]. Hence, consumers and tourists now play an active role in shaping an organization's reputation [13], which in turn can impact the organisation's sales performance [36]. Therefore, the analysis of reviews has become a mainstream activity in marketing to improve product and services positioning based on

© Springer Nature Switzerland AG 2020
S. Dupuy-Chessa and H. A. Proper (Eds.): CAiSE 2020 Workshops, LNBIP 382, pp. 95–108, 2020.
https://doi.org/10.1007/978-3-030-49165-9_9

customers' needs and opinions [18]. According to [28], a brand is no longer what the company tells a customer it is, but rather, what customers tell each other it is.

TripAdvisor and other social media platforms have become valuable sources of eWOM in the tourism domain, with several studies investigating sentiment in reviews [27] given evidence that it can predict product success [29]. Topic modelling has also been used to identify topics discussed in reviews to provide temporal associations between topics in a timeline. These studies, however, concentrated on endogenous aspects of tourists' reviews (i.e., sentiment) whilst exogenous aspects, such as culture and purchasing power, have been addressed separately. No study so far combines exogenous with endogenous variables in one model to investigate the reasons for tourist dissatisfaction and predict perspective tourists' sentiment. Therefore, this paper investigates the application of Decision Trees to identify patterns, by evaluating the combined effect of culture, purchasing power, and topics discussed by tourists in reviews, on sentiment polarity. The research questions addressed in this paper are: (i) What are the main patterns emerging from tourist reviews of Cyprus hotels? (ii) How endogenous and exogenous reviews' parameters affect tourist sentiment?

The paper is organized as follows. Section 2 reviews the literature pertaining to the effect of culture and purchasing power on tourists' experience. Sections 3 and 4 elaborate on the proposed methodology and the obtained results, respectively. The paper concludes with the implications of the research and future directions.

2   Literature Review

The literature related to culture and purchasing power is presented next.

2.1   Culture

The driver to address culture within our research question is grounded on evidence that the tourists' cultural values, such as power distance, individualism, and uncertainty avoidance, significantly affect their perception of service quality, service evaluation, and satisfaction [20] Other studies indicate that the customers' power distance significantly affects their service expectations, perceived service quality, and relationship quality [10]. A key factor that differentiates tourist activities at a destination is culture, with studies, e.g. [8], identifying that certain traits have significant differences. This theory is also supported in consumer behaviour by evidence showing that people of the same nationality tend to have similar preferences [16].

There are several models of culture. In this study, we adopted the model of Hofstede [14] due to its eminent reputation. According to this model, there are six different traits that form a culture: (1) *Power Distance* (i.e. the degree to which people accept and expect that power is distributed unequally); (2) *Individualism* (i.e. the degree to which people tend to take care of only themselves and their immediate families); (3) *Masculinity* (i.e. the degree to which achievement, heroism, assertiveness, and material rewards for success are preferred); (4)*Uncertainty Avoidance* (i.e. the degree to which risk and uncertainty tend to be avoided; (5) *Long Term Orientation* (i.e. the degree to which people prefer stability, respect for tradition, and are future-oriented);

and (6) *Indulgence* (i.e. the degree to which people prefer freedom and free will). For the purpose of this study, we used Hofstede's cross-cultural differences model (similar to [16]) to obtain each reviewer's culture values to enhance our tourist review data.

2.2 Purchasing Power

The use of purchasing power is grounded on evidence highlighting that customers from countries with greater power distance feel superior to service providers [20] and expect high service quality. This is linked to evidence that purchasing power [38] is linked with a greater need to portray status through consumption [12], hence promoting power distance. The financial state of a country has been used for global markets analysis [15] with Gross Domestic Product (GDP) per capita as a key indicator for comparing the level of development among countries and socioeconomic status. Human welfare and GDP per capita go together, while increased GDP per capita is found to be correlated with happiness [11]. At the same time, in countries with low human development index, GDP dramatically affects quality of life [17]. Therefore, the argument by many researchers is that tourists from countries with lower purchasing power compared to their tourist destination might be more demanding and hence more likely to evaluate their experience at a destination negatively.

3 Methodology

The techniques used to address our research questions include sentiment analysis, topic modelling, decision trees, and imbalance data treatment. These are described in turn along with the overall proposed methodology that combines them.

3.1 Sentiment Analysis

Sentiment analysis (SA) and opinion mining have been studied and used for a while with several techniques emerging for analysing emotions and opinions from eWOM [26]. SA is useful for online opinions analysis due to its ability to automatically measure emotion in online content using algorithms to detect polarity in eWOM [32]. Three common SA approaches are Machine Learning (ML), Lexicon-based Methods, and Linguistic Analysis techniques. From these ML techniques are considered the most effective and simplest to use with Naïve Bayes (NB) and Support Vector Machines (SVM) being the most popular. ML techniques are classified into supervised and unsupervised [41], with supervised requiring training the classifier prior to its use. The main difference from unsupervised is that supervised techniques use labelled opinions that have been pre-evaluated as negative, positive, or neutral to train models. Such techniques include SVM, NB, Logistic Regression, Multilayer Perceptron, K-Nearest Neighbours, and Decision Trees [23]. In this study, the NB approach is employed for SA due to its good results and popularity [3, 24, 39].

3.2   Topic Modelling

Topic modelling, a type of unsupervised data mining technique, constitutes a popular tool for extracting important themes (topics) from unstructured data and is employed to reveal and annotate large documents collection with thematic information [31]. Two of the most popular techniques for topic analysis are the Latent Dirichlet Allocation (LDA) and the Structural Topic Model (STM) [14]. In LDA, a topic is a probability distribution function over a set of words used as a type of text summarization. LDA expresses the relationships between words in terms of their affinity to certain latent variables (topics), using Bayesian probabilities. STMs extend the LDA framework with the capability of accommodating supplementary information in the form of metadata that could reveal important aspects of how topics are linked to covariates [35], or to observe which topics correlate with one another [9]. LDA and STM are generative models and assume that each topic is a distribution over words and each document is a mixture of topics [7]. STM is employed in this study, with each review representing a distribution of a finite set of topics, which in turn are distributions of the words in the corpus used in similar reviews. Identified topics were later associated to each review in the dataset. New columns are added depending on the number of topics, each representing the degree of association of each topic to the case.

3.3   Decision Trees

Decision Trees (DT) are considered a scalable multivariate method and have been successfully applied in prediction problems by mimicking the human decision-making process. They are intuitive and explanatory, unlike black-box algorithms such as support vector machines or artificial neural networks that cannot be easily comprehended by decision makers or validated by domain experts. A DT learns its structure by partitioning the training dataset into bins using a series of splits, each performed after identifying the most prevalent split-variable using information gain or Gini impurity index metrics. Splitting variables are used in defining the structure of the tree that is made up of nodes. Each node splits the dataset into branches. There are several algorithms for designing DTs such as CART, ID3, C4.5, CHAID etc. The CART algorithm [5] is a binary classification technique that utilises the Gini index of heterogeneity to determine the information gain of each variable and accordingly decide which variables to be used to split the dataset.

The main advantages of DTs lie in their simple interpretation and visualization capabilities, and the need for little data preparation. They can handle both numerical and categorical data. Their drawbacks include creation of over-complex trees that could sometimes overfit the data and not generalize well. This is due to the use of heuristic algorithms such as the greedy algorithm, where locally optimal decisions are made at each node. Another drawback is that DT algorithms create biased trees if the training set is imbalanced (large difference in number of cases representing the class variable). It is, thus, recommended to balance the dataset as explained next, prior to DT training.

Hyperparameter tuning is another activity performed prior to model learning to find the optimum configuration of a DT for improved model performance. There is no uniform way to specify hyperparameter values to reduce the loss of model performance; experimentation through a grid-based search is a common approach. However, supervised algorithms can be used to automate this process. The main parameters utilized in this study to optimize the performance of the DT was the alpha value (DT cost complexity), the DT maximum depth, and minimum samples per leaf node [25].

3.4   Data Balancing

Data imbalance refers to the situation when the minority class of a dataset is much smaller than the majority class. In our case, the number of positive sentiment reviews was much larger than the negative ones (minority). This class imbalance can mislead the classifier into overfitting, since the majority class dominates the dataset. Hence, the classifier always generates results that abide with the majority class. Solutions to the class-imbalance problem include many different forms of under-sampling or over-sampling. The oversampling approach creates a balanced subset from the original dataset by duplicating samples of the minority class. Two of the most common oversampling techniques are Random oversampling (RO) and the Synthetic Minority Oversampling Technique (SMOTE). RO is easy to implement and involves the minority samples in the data being replicated randomly until the proportion of majority class is achieved. The SMOTE technique generates artificial samples from the minority class by combining several minority-class instances that are similar. That is, for each minority instance, it introduces a synthetic new sample by utilizing information from the minority-class nearest-neighbours instances. SMOTE is a more sophisticated technique and generally produces better results [40] than RO. We implemented and tested both approaches, confirming SMOTE's superior performance. Hence, SMOTE was employed to balance the training dataset before generating the DT model.

3.5   Overall Methodology

The main steps required to answer our research questions are depicted in Fig. 1. The first step is the collection of reviews, in English, from tourists who visited hotels in Cyprus during the period 2009-2019. This period is selected due to availability of data. The total number of reviews obtained from the data collection is 65000 from tourists representing 27 countries with the majority (85%) of cases representing years 2014-2019 due to the recent increase in eWOM popularity. Data was automatically extracted from TripAdvisor, with an algorithm developed in python that scrapped the reviews, and included: Username, Rating of hotel, Date of stay, Feedback date, Country of origin, Past contributions, Confidence votes, Review. To estimate each country's purchasing power, the GDP per capita index was used, using data from the World Monetary Fund. The variable is expressed in US dollars and was standardized in a scale from 0 to 100. Similarly, for the cultural values of each reviewer, the Hofstede website was used, associating each cultural dimension to a value in a scale from 0-100, based on country of origin. The tourists' reviews, GDP, and culture data were integrated to form a collated dataset used for DT training.

Prior to DT training, the data underwent cleansing, dimensionality reduction, and irrelevant data elimination. Cases with missing values (i.e., culture values) were

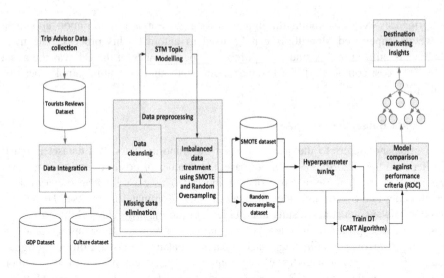

Fig. 1. Overall methodology

eliminated from the dataset, reducing the number of cases to 45000. The next step involved the analysis of consumers' sentiment and the topics discussed in the reviews, through polarity detection and topic analysis, respectively.

For the sentiment analysis, a pre-trained NB classifier was used, to evaluate the polarity of reviews initially in three categories: positive, negative, and neutral. The rationale for using a sentiment classifier instead of the actual review's rating in Trip Advisor, lies in evidence [22] suggesting that reviewers tend to refrain from giving low scores to hotels unless their experience is extremely negative. In this study [22] for instance they examined whether reviewers from collectivist-leaning societies (valuing tradition and helping each other) tend to write fewer excessively negative reviews than those from individualistic societies. They found that despite being marginally positive in ratings, reviewers use negative connotations in narrative descriptions that indicate dissatisfaction. To avoid this problem, we opted for a sentiment classification approach rather than using the reviewer's ratings alone. The two trained sentiment models used for this task were Textblob (based on Naive Bayes) and Vader [17], which are popular classifiers with satisfactory precision and recall scores. Both models were used in an ensemble manner to improve our confidence in the results. A python script automatically utilized the Textblob and Vader models and averaged their results. The process was repeated for all downloaded reviews, and their polarity was saved next to each review as a new attribute.

To reduce the data imbalance (5% negative, 10% neutral, and 85% positive), the sentiment polarity was converted to a binary state by merging the neutral and negative sentiments. This assumes that neutral sentiment is closer to the negative than the positive class due to reluctance of people giving negative reviews. This resulted in 15-85 data distribution, which was still imbalanced and was tackled in a subsequent step.

An additional issue that needed addressing prior to DT model learning was the fact that many of the reviews were from UK tourists. These represented 70% of the dataset that monopolised the GDP and culture scores. Therefore, to minimize the bias from this majority group, a random sample was selected from the UK group to equate the maximum number of reviews from other tourists' groups. The resulting dataset included a total of 10,3K reviews.

The STM topic modelling approach is subsequently used to associate reviews with key thematic topics identified from the whole dataset. To learn the topic model, reviews had to be pre-processed further. During this step, irrelevant information was eliminated through the sub-steps of stop-word removal, tokenization, stemming. Stop-words refer to words providing little or no useful information to text analysis and can hence be considered as noise. Common stop-words include articles, conjunctions, prepositions and pronouns. Tokenization refers to the transformation of a stream of strings into a stream of processing units, referred to as tokens. Thus, during this step reviews were converted into a sequence of tokens, by choosing n-grams (phrases composed by n words in length). The Stemming process involves converting words to their root form. After data pre-processing, the STM topic modelling approach was employed. Extracted topics were inspected based on prior domain knowledge; therefore, expertise in the field under investigation was required to make the necessary connections. The identification of the recommended number of topics (k) was based on the model's semantic coherence and exclusivity for each model and topic [35]. The recommended value for k from this process was 10. Manual inspection of the resulting topics followed to identify possible topic merges into super-topics to reduce the dimensionality of the model further. This yielded the six super-topics of Table 2. Each review was then associated with super-topics based on the results of the trained model and the topic merges. The super-topic associations were appended as new variables in the datafile based on the probability distribution of topics per review, i.e., each review is associated with more than one topic.

To tackle the data imbalance challenge, the dataset that emerged from the super-topic assignment underwent treatment using SMOTE and RO techniques, yielding two new datasets that were utilized during DT training. Hyperparameter tuning was performed to identify the best configuration of the DT learning algorithm (CART) to maximize the model's performance. To validate the generated DTs from the SMOTE and RO datasets, the K-fold cross-validation approach was used. The Area Under the Receiver Operating Characteristic (ROC) curve (AUC), used for binary classification problems such as this one (pos/neg sentiment), describes the performance of a model as a whole and is useful for evaluating models trained on imbalanced data [4]. The higher the area under the ROC curve the better the model's performance. The best model was obtained using the SMOTE dataset with AUC 81.9%, while the DT generated from the RO dataset was inferior (78%) due to replicating existing cases from minority class.

The learned DT is finally used to identify the most significant patterns in the dataset. These are expressed as rules that combine both exogenous and endogenous variables of tourists' reviews and are indicated as nodes on the tree. Nodes also provide information concerning the polarity and are color-coded accordingly. The key rules are subsequently used to filter cases from the dataset that satisfy the rules, which are then used to estimate the distribution of tourists by country of origin. Countries with higher probabilities in each rules' sample-set, represent tourist origins that are more likely to be satisfied by existing services at a tourist destination. Such information can provide interesting marketing insights to be used by destination managers to identify the things they do well or badly, and accordingly tailor their campaigns knowing which groups they can satisfy better.

4 Results

The first analytical step was the identification of the main topics discussed in the corpus of tourists' reviews. The STM method was used, and the recommended number of topics was identified to be ten based on the topic coherence, which denotes whether words in the same topic make sense when they are put together. The 10 topics identified are depicted in Table 1 along with the distribution of words for each topic. The table shows the most popular words that comprise each topic using different metrics such as highest probability, FREX, Lift, and Score. FREX weights words by their overall frequency and how exclusive they are to the topic, while Lift weights words by giving higher weight to words that appear less frequently in other topics. Score divides the log frequency of the word in the topic by the log frequency of the word in other topics. Based on these scores, words are presented in order from left to right, indicating their importance to the topic. The right column presents the interpretation of the topic in domain specific language.

To minimize the complexity of the topic model, the generated topics were merged into six super-topics based on common themes specified in Table 2. The last column in Table 2 provides the meaning of a high score for a super-topic. For example, a high cleanliness score indicates many complains about the cleanness of the hotel, while a high services/staff score indicates high satisfaction with the staff.

The DT classification task using the compiled data revealed that the combined use of the three predictor variables (culture, GDP per capita, super-topics) were able to predict group membership (reviews' sentiment polarity) better than chance (50/50) with overall prediction accuracy of 80%. The optimal decision tree is presented in Fig. 2. Each node depicts the state of each of the variables with super-topics expressed as a percentage with zero indicating no discussions about a topic and 100 many discussions. The values in each tree node denote the number of cases from the dataset that satisfy a given node criterion. The values on the left correspond to negative sentiment cases and the values on the right with positive. The Gini index (calculated by subtracting the sum of the squared probabilities of each class from one) shows the level of impurity of the distribution for each node with lower index indicating a larger difference between negative and positive sentiment. This is also visually represented using colour coding for the tree nodes. The Gini index is utilised to identify strong patterns in the dataset that are expressed in the form of rules.

The dominating variable in this tree is the topic associated with cleanliness followed by service and staff professionalism. High cleanliness issues (cleanliness > 20.5), indicating a lot of complains about cleanliness, yield 91% negative reviews (computed based on negative cases over total cases on the leaf node). This abides with results from [37]. However, when mild cleanliness is combined with high professional staff attitude (Service/Staff > 12.5), the reviews are slightly positive

Table 1. Emerging topics from STA and their interpretation

Topic	Top words per topic from STA based on four metrics	Interpretation
1	Highest Prob: room, hotel, bathroom, one, bed, shower, water FREX: shower, toilet, smell, window, eggs, air, bathroom Lift: toast, electric, scrambled, curtain, soap, ham, conditioner Score: toast, room, shower, bathroom, air, toilet, dirty	Cleanness of hotel and rooms
2	Highest Prob: hotel, staff, great, service, will, time, best FREX: wonderful, thank, amazing, thanks, vacation, highly, come Lift: die, wonderfull, pampered, costas, thanks, thank, surely Score: die, amazing, hotel, thank, great, staff, perfect	Service/Staff
3	Highest Prob: kids, restaurant, pool, well, pools, every, day FREX: resort, kids, club, gardens, chef, activities, adults Lift: elias, tranquility, exotic, azia, treatments, slides, dome Score: elias, kids, resort, team, pools, children, spa	Family friendly
4	Highest Prob: good, breakfast, hotel, room, rooms, clean, staff FREX: breakfast, comfortable, modern, view, spacious, rooms, wifi Lift: wonderfully, modern, satisfactory, spread, amphora, comfortable Score: wonderfully, good, breakfast, room, rooms, clean, comfortable	Breakfast and overall quality
5	Highest Prob: place, stay, stayed, cyprus, apartment, night, everything FREX: apartment, owner, apartments, place, accommodation, budget Lift: scale, asty, pyramos, san, remo, owner, apt Score: scale, place, apartment, apartments, stay, nicosia, owner	Budget stay
6	Highest Prob: hotel, food, dinner, get, day, evening, drinks FREX: board, half, drinks, eat, bay, lunch, inclusive Lift: famagusta, casino, brits, salamis, ajax, potatoes, Turkish Score: famagusta, half, entertainment, euro, board, food, inclusive	All-inclusive food
7	Highest Prob: hotel, room, day, didnt, one, got, night FREX: told, said, wasnt, didnt, asked, got, never Lift: paint, veronica, upset, sorted, complaining, dirt, realised Score: paint, told, didnt, said, asked, never, got	Complains about room

(*continued*)

Table 1. (*continued*)

Topic	Top words per topic from STA based on four metrics	Interpretation
8	Highest Prob: hotel, walk, bus, minutes, beach, restaurants, larnaca FREX: walking, distance, bus, street, shops, walk, minutes Lift: route, mackenzie, cafes, intercity, lazarus, sights, mall Score: route, bus, walk, street, distance, city, larnaca	Hotel location and things to do
9	Highest Prob: hotel, guests, hotels, star, one, well, area FREX: guests, seasons, standards, four, management, star, years Lift: miserable, allows, result, wonâ, greatly, thoughtful, post Score: miserable, guests, seasons, star, years, four, management	Other guests
10	Highest Prob: nice, pool, beach, hotel, good, really, great FREX: napa, nice, ayia, pool, really, swimming, plaza Lift: pleasent, swiming, plaza, nestor, napa, ayia, aya Score: pleasent, nice, pool, napa, beach, great, good	Beach hotel and pool

Table 2. Super-topics that emerged from topic combinations and score interpretations

Topics with overlapping themes	Interpretation	High score meaning
Topic 1,7	Cleanliness	Complains
Topic 3,10, 6, 4	Family/Pool/Food	Satisfaction
Topic 5	Budget	Budget hotel
Topic 8	Location	Good location
Topic 2	Service/Staff	Satisfaction
Topic 9	Other Guests	High mixture of guest cultures

(67%). Staff professionalism and quality of service is a strong predictor of positive reviews with a weight of 93%, result also supported by [37].

Issues with multicultural guests (other guests) emerge with hotel guests from different cultures interacting in a hotel, combined with low staff satisfaction, leading to 81% negative reviews. An important cultural dimension that yields negative sentiment when the hotel service is not adequate is Power distance with a 65% weight on negative reviews. Low indulgence (indicating control of desires) yields positive sentiment in 71% of the cases when no cleanliness and staff issues are encountered, while the combination of high indulgence with low GDP per capita results in marginally negative sentiment, indicating that tourist from poorer countries who want to satisfy their desires

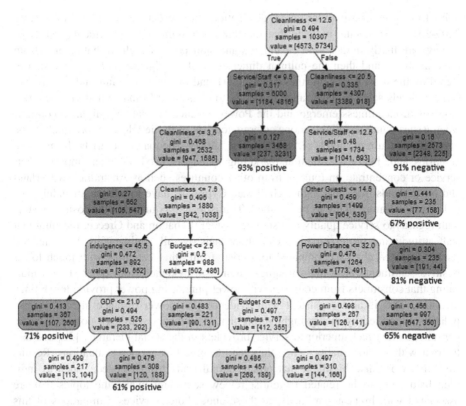

Fig. 2. Learned Decision Tree with colour coded sentiment predictions (negative shown in shades of orange and positive in shades of blue). Key results are annotated under the leafs. (Color figure online)

expect more for their money. On the other hand, tourists from richer countries tend to give positive sentiment in 61% of cases. Preliminary evaluation of the model's most prevalent patterns was performed using comparative analysis with relevant literature. Studies on cleanliness, service [37], and value for money (GDP) [30] report a similar effect on satisfaction. The latter is similar to our GDP dimension and utilises equity theory [1] to observe that satisfaction is occurring when the performance of the service equates the money paid for the service. The model was further evaluated by two experts from the hospitality industry who verified the validity of these rules.

5 Conclusions

This study serves as a proof-of-concept and is the first to combine a DT approach with topic modelling to identify patterns using both exogenous and endogenous parameters of tourists' reviews. Several studies examined mainly the impact of culture on review generation [21, 22, 34], therefore this work provides a contribution by combining other exogenous and endogenous variables. The case study used to elaborate this method refers to Cyprus as a popular tourist destination and the data collected span the years 2009-2019. The results indicate that the three determinants of sentiment polarity in reviews are firstly, issues with cleanliness and staff professionalism that emerge from topic analysis, and then the cultural dimensions of indulgence and power distance. Based on the most prevalent rules from the DT and the cases that fall under each one, Cypriot hotels seem to have failed to satisfy tourists from Romania and Greece when issues with cleanliness emerge and the Power distance is relatively high. In contrast, when issues with Cleanliness alone emerge, tourists from the UK are more likely to be dissatisfied. Current hotel services cannot satisfy adequately tourists from these countries and, hence, destination marketing managers need to either improve their service or concentrate on tourists from other countries such as Australia, Switzerland and Netherlands that have higher GDP than Cyprus or have low levels of indulgence (<45) and are more likely to be satisfied. Tourist origin countries with positive results with regards to service quality and staff are, Israel, Lebanon and Greece, meaning that staff attitude and professionalism can affect their overall sentiment by 12% and 8% (Israel, Greece/Lebanon) compared to tourists from other countries with much lower positive sentiments. The main findings align with evidence from other studies indicating that consumers from countries with lower purchasing power provide low ratings to hotels. This is also consistent with evidence that power distance affects reviews polarity, supported by theory highlighting that in countries with high power distance, consumers often feel superior to service providers in the social hierarchy [20] and less tolerant with service quality, while they tend to give low service evaluations. Results from this work also highlight that other cultural traits from Hofstede, such as individualism, tend to be related to tourist review sentiment, while the topics that are associated with highest sentiment are those about hotel services. Limitations of this work reside in the quality of the data collected and issues pertaining to fake reviews that might affect the results. Our future work aims to filter out these reviews and examine if the effect of the aforementioned variables alters in any way the main conclusions of the current study.

References

1. Adams, J.S.: Towards an understanding of inequity. J. Abnorm. Soc. Psychol. **67**(5), 422 (1963)
2. Berger, J., Milkman, K.: What Makes Online Content Viral? J. Mark. Res. **49**, 192–205 (2012)
3. Boiy, E., Moens, M.F.: A machine learning approach to sentiment analysis in multilingual web texts. Inf. Retr. **12**(5), 526–558 (2009)
4. Bradley, A.P.: The use of the area under the ROC curve in the evaluation of machine learning algorithms. Patt. Recogn. **30**(7), 1145–1159 (1997)
5. Breiman, L., Friedman, J., Stone, C., Olshen, R.: Classification and Regression Trees (Wadsworth Statistics/Probability). CRC Press, New York (1984)
6. Chamlertwat, W., Bhattarakosol, P., Rungkasiri, T., Haruechaiyasak, C.: Discovering consumer insight from Twitter via sentiment analysis. J. Uni. Comput. Sci. **18**, 973–992 (2012)

7. Chaney, A.J.B., Blei, D.M.: Visualizing topic models. In: ICWSM 2012 - Proceedings of the 6th International AAAI Conference on Weblogs and Social Media (2012)
8. Crotts, J., Erdmann, R.: Does national culture influence consumers' evaluation of travel services? A test of Hofstede's model of cross-cultural differences. MSQ **10**, 410–419 (2000)
9. Csardi, G., Nepusz, T.: The igraph software package for complex network research. Inter J. Complex Syst. **1695**, 1–9 (2006)
10. Dash, S., Bruning, E., Acharya, M.: The effect of power distance and individualism on service quality expectations in banking: a two-country individual- and national-cultural comparison. Int. J. Bank Mark. **27**, 336–358 (2009)
11. Dipietro, W.R., Anoruo, E.: GDP per capita and its challengers as measures of happiness. Int. J. Soc. Econ. **33**, 698–709 (2006)
12. Dubois, B., Duquesne, P.: The market for luxury goods: income versus culture. Eur. J. Mark. **27**, 35–44 (1993)
13. Etter, M., Ravasi, D., Colleoni, E.: Social media and the formation of organizational reputation. Acad. Manag. Rev. **44**, 28–52 (2019)
14. Gambhir, M., Gupta, V.: Recent automatic text summarization techniques: a survey. Artif. Intell. Rev. **47**, 1–66 (2017)
15. Gilboa, S., Mitchell, V.: The role of culture and purchasing power parity in shaping mall-shoppers' profiles. J. Retail. Consum. Serv. **52** (2020)
16. Huang, S., Crotts, J.: Relationships between Hofstede's cultural dimensions and tourist satisfaction: a cross-country cross-sample examination. Tour. Manag. **52**, 232–241 (2019)
17. Hutto, C.J., Gilbert, E.: VADER: a parsimonious rule-based model for sentiment analysis of social media text. In: ICWSM (2014)
18. Jung, J.J.: Taxonomy alignment for interoperability between heterogeneous virtual organizations. Exp. Syst. Appl. **34**, 2721–2731 (2008)
19. Khade, A.A.: Performing customer behavior analysis using big data analytics. Procedia Comput. Sci. **79**, 986–992 (2016)
20. Kim, C.S., Aggarwal, P.: The customer is king: culture-based unintended consequences of modern marketing. J. Consum. Mark. **33**, 193–201 (2016)
21. Kim, J.M., Jun, M., Kim, C.K.: The effects of culture on consumers' consumption and generation of online reviews. J. Interact. Mark. **43**, 134–150 (2018)
22. Koh, N.S., Hu, N., Clemons, E.K.: Do online reviews reflect a product's true perceived quality? an investigation of online movie reviews across cultures. ECRA **9**, 374–385 (2010)
23. Krouska, A., Troussas, C., Virvou, M.: Comparative evaluation of algorithms for sentiment analysis over social networking services. J. Univ. Comput. Sci. **23**, 755–768 (2017)
24. Liu, B.: Sentiment analysis and opinion mining. Synth. Lect. Hum. Lang. Technol. (2012)
25. Mantovani, R.G., Horvath, T., Cerri. R., Vanschoren, J., De Carvalho, A.C.P.L.F.: Hyper-parameter tuning of a decision tree induction algorithm. In: BRACIS (2016)
26. Martin-Domingo, L., Martín, J.C., Mandsberg, G.: Social media as a resource for sentiment analysis of Airport Service Quality (ASQ). J. Air. Transp. Manag. **78**, 106–115 (2019)
27. Moon, S., Kamakura, W.A.: A picture is worth a thousand words: translating product reviews into a product positioning map. Int. J. Res. Mark. **34**, 265–285 (2017)
28. Nayab, G., Bilal, M., Shrafat, A.: A brand is no longer what we tell the customer it is - it is what customers tell each other it is: (Lahome). Sci. Int. **28**, 2725–2729 (2016)
29. Nguyen, H., Chaudhuri, M.: Making new products go viral and succd. IJRM **36**, 39–62 (2019)
30. Nicolau, J.L., Mellinas, J.P., Martín-Fuentes, E.: Satisfaction measures with monetary and non-monetary components: hotel's overall scores. Int. J. Hosp. Manag. **87**, 102497 (2020)
31. Nikolenko, S.I., Koltcov, S., Koltsova, O.: Topic modelling for qualitative studies. J. Inf. Sci. **43**, 88–102 (2017)

32. Pang, B., Lee, L.: Opinion mining and sentiment analysis. FT Inf. Retr. **2**, 1–135 (2008)
33. Pfeffer, J., Zorbach, T., Carley, K,M.: Understanding online firestorms: negative word-of-mouth dynamics in social media networks. J. Mark. Commun. **20**, 117–128 (2014)
34. Purnawirawan, N., Eisend, M., De Pelsmacker, P., Dens, N.: A meta-analytic investigation of the role of valence in online reviews. J. Interact. Mark. **31**, 17–27 (2015)
35. Roberts, M., et al.: Structural topic models for open-ended survey responses. AJPS **58**, 1064–1082 (2014)
36. Rosario, A., Sotgiu, F., De Valck, K., Bijmolt, T.: The effect of eWOM on sales: a meta-analytic review of platform, product, and metric factors. J. Mark. Res. **53**, 297–318 (2016)
37. Sann, R., Lai, P.C., Liaw, S.Y.: Online complaining behavior: does cultural background and hotel class matter? J. Hosp. Tour. Manag. **43**, 80–90 (2020)
38. Schaninger, C.M.: Social class versus income revisited: an empirical investigation. J. Mark. Res. **18**, 192–208 (1981)
39. Singh, V.K., Piryani, R., Uddin, A., Waila, P.M.: Sentiment analysis of textual reviews; Evaluating machine learning, unsupervised and SentiWordNet approaches (2013)
40. Thabtah, F., Hammoud, S., Kamalov, F., Gonsalves, A.: Data imbalance in classification: experimental evaluation. Inf. Sci. (Ny) (2020)
41. Witten, I.H., Frank, E., Hall, M.A., Pal, C.J.: Data Mining: Practical Machine Learning Tools and Techniques. Elsevier, Amsterdam (2011)

Social *Participation* Network: Linking Things, Services and People to Support Participatory Processes

Grigorios Piperagkas[1], Rafael Angarita[2(✉)], and Valérie Issarny[1]

[1] Inria, Paris, France
{grigorios.piperagkas,valerie.issarny}@inria.fr
[2] ISEP, Paris, France
rafael.angarita@isep.paris

Abstract. Digital technologies have impacted almost every aspect of our society, including how people participate in activities that matter to them. Indeed, digital participation allows people to be involved in different societal activities at an unprecedented scale through the use of Information and Communication Technologies (ICT). Still, enabling participation at scale requires making it seamless for people to: interact with a variety of software platforms, get information from connected physical objects and software services, and communicate and collaborate with their peers. Toward this objective, this paper introduces and formalizes the concept of *Social Participation Network*, which captures the diverse *participation relationships* – between people, digital services and connected things – supporting participatory processes. The paper further presents the early design of an associated online service to support the creation and management of Social *Participation* Networks. The design advocates the instantiation of Social *Participation* Networks within distinct participation contexts—spanning, e.g., private institutions, neighbor communities, and governmental institutions—so that the participants' information and contributions to participation remain isolated and private within the given context.

Keywords: Social networks · Internet of Things · Participatory technologies · Rule-based systems · Ontology

1 Introduction

An increasing number of institutions and self-organized communities have been promoting the use of information and communication technologies (ICT) to improve the participation of people in community-wide processes as diverse as, e.g., online education, neighborhood projects, or public consultation. Such digitally-powered participation, known as *digital participation* [24], has led to the emergence of various participatory practices that empower people at scale. Illustrative examples include: crowd-sourcing/-funding [14], participatory budgeting [15], peer to peer sharing in communities [26], open government data

© Springer Nature Switzerland AG 2020
S. Dupuy-Chessa and H. A. Proper (Eds.): CAiSE 2020 Workshops, LNBIP 382, pp. 109–120, 2020.
https://doi.org/10.1007/978-3-030-49165-9_10

access & analysis [25], participatory urban planning [6], and public consultations [21].

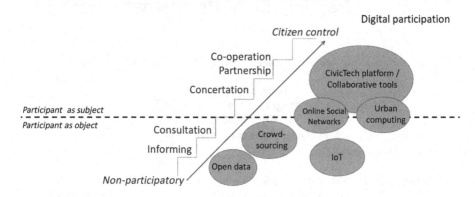

Fig. 1. Ladder of Participation and supporting technologies.

As the "*Ladder of Participation*" illustrates [4], there exist different levels of involvement of the community in participatory processes, from *non-participatory* to *citizen control*, through to, e.g., *informing*, *consultation* and *partnership*. Still, independent of the target level of participation, enabling digital participation requires making it seamless for people to connect and interact with the relevant community of people but also of digital entities (see Fig. 1). Indeed, the "community" of digital entities is essential to support the implementation of participatory processes in the digital world and even in the physical world by way of the IoT. Toward that direction, this paper introduces the concept of *Social Participation Network*, which captures the various entities that may potentially engage in a given digital participatory process, while abstracting the underlying heterogeneity.

In what follows, we first walk through illustrative examples of participation that have flourished in the digital society over the last ten years, from the government-led top-down to the people-led bottom-up approaches (Sect. 2). Then, using a dedicated ontology, we define the digital entities and relations among them that a *Social Participation Network* characterizes (Sect. 3). We also introduce the rules that govern the emergence of relationships among the participating entities within a network to enhance the associated participatory process, while enforcing privacy and security guarantees to participants. We then present the early design of an online service – introducing its architecture and component technologies – supporting the implementation of participatory processes based on the proposed concept of *Social Participation Network* (Sect. 4). Finally, we conclude with a summary of our contribution and the research challenges ahead of us (Sect. 5).

2   Digital Participation: A Socio-Technical Perspective

The development of participatory technologies has been drastic over the last ten years, as it builds upon the development of ICT and their increasing widespread adoption by the masses. We may classify the related participatory initiatives according to who is leading them: government, people or both.

Government-Led Initiatives: *Open government* promotes governmental transparency and accountability, so as to reduce democratic malfunctioning incidents. *Open data* is among the pioneer implementation of open government in today's digital era. Still, there exist various implementations of the concept [16], which differ according to the level of participation, from the citizen being a mere consumer to an actor, of the government actions. Accordingly, a number of software tools support the open data movement, from the management of data to engaging developers in the creation of new applications as *Open Government Data as a Service* illustrates [20]. The proper organization of the exposed data is in particular essential to avoid misinterpretations and requires appropriate visualization tools. Still in the direction of leveraging digital technologies for opening up government knowledge and practices, agencies have applied *crowdsourcing* to foster civic participation at a massive scale for top-down politics, reform discussion and e-voting. Examples are many and include: the constitution reform in Iceland [17], open ministry in Finland [8] and open innovation strategies [7]. According to Aitamurto [1], crowdsourcing with co-creation constitutes the main method for realizing participatory democracy.

The analysis of practices and associated digital tools supporting the "open government" approach shows that they ignore too often the fundamental principles of effective deliberation, participation and collaboration, and focus mainly on transparency and information [13]. People-led initiatives fostering actions at the community level tend to overcome the shortcomings.

People-Led Community Actions: *Social media* are a tool of choice for communities of people to organize themselves. This includes using well-established *Online Social Networks* (OSNs) for political discussion and online deliberation [12]. Existing studies of this specific use of OSNs further suggest the design of OSN services dedicated to political organization and action. This is to foster online interactions that have shown to play a crucial role in the formation of a movement, where politics is obvious to everyday life, in contrast to formal settings [9]. The emergence of specialized *community social media* sustains well the analysis. The associated software applications then serve connecting the residents of a given local community via an exclusive portal, further implementing strong features for building trust and safety among users.

It is worth stressing that the society's digitization allows for people-led actions at a large scale. The Web-based *We Europeans*[1] civic consultation is one such illustration. The consultation, run between February and March 2019, allowed European citizens to offer solutions on concrete steps to be taken to

---

[1] https://weeuropeans.eu.

reinvent Europe. The initiative collected 30,000 proposals and 1,7 million votes. The top 10 proposals of each country were then translated in all the European languages, so that European citizens could vote in a second round to identify the top 10 proposals at the European level. Finally, the political parties of every country were able to take a stand on these proposals and share their position via the *We Europeans* Web application.

Hybrid Urban-Scale Actions: The most common form of people participation is urban-centric. With the development of computing in urban environments and of the smart city vision, participatory platforms have been gaining momentum. These platforms and associated applications ease and organize the interactions of the connected people among them and/or with local authorities and agencies. They also promote collective actions.

Urban computing is at the heart of the development of urban applications. As defined in [28], urban computing *is a process of acquisition, integration, and analysis of big and heterogeneous data generated by diverse sources in urban spaces, such as sensors, devices, vehicles, buildings, and humans, to tackle major issues that cities face.* The supporting software platforms then cope with: sensing and data collection, analyzing the data, and combining the physical with the virtual environments (i.e., social networking and sensor data integration). As such, the software solutions involve a large diversity of systems, spanning: mobile computing, cyber-physical, and Artificial Intelligence, to name a few. The widespread adoption of smartphones and further development of the IoT, allow collecting data that address multiple domains of the smart cities – mobility, health, utilities, *etc.* – and offer a unique opportunity for participatory applications. This includes accommodating political expression and participation. Fostering massive participation then becomes the target in the deployment of applications in the wild [23], while the abundance and complexity of applications ultimately lead to lessen the interactions with people and among them. However, development in the area of civic technologies (aka *Civic Tech*) aims at offering platforms easing participatory processes at scale although introducing proprietary technologies that limit their adoption.

3   Social Participation Networks: Connecting the Actors of Participation

The previous section illustrates the key role of Cyber-Physical-Social Systems (CPSS) in the realization of digital participatory processes: People not solely need to network together, they also need the digital tools to collaborate, get access to the relevant information and (co-)create. We argue that the specific *participatory CPSS* must be structured around the paradigm of *social participation network* that manages the connection of people, actions and digital entities according to their relevance to the focus of the participation. The paradigm of social participation network builds upon the well known one of OSN and of the more recent *social IoT* [5]. The latter aims at integrating social networking concepts into the Internet of Things (IoT). That is, the social IoT creates social network graphs of people and things, in which the relations with things derive from the things' ownership and physical properties. The distinctive feature of a *social participation network* is then to specifically manage *participatory links* among people and digital entities so as to enable:

- People to *connect* with other people who share similar interests within a given group, thereby enabling the social character of participation.
- People to *discover* the participatory actions in which they are interested and may engage in online and/or offline.
- Digital entities – associated with the participants and/or the actions – to *discover* and *connect* with each other, thereby automating supporting actions (e.g., information sharing).

The structure of a *social participation network* underlying a participatory process evolves as the participants come and go, and their contributions and interests change over the course of the process. Table 1 illustrates **events** and **operations** that instigate changes to *social participation networks*, while we focus on the case of the network expansion in the paper. *Events* are fired by the participating human and cyber actors (e.g., a person showing interest in a theme, a new device providing observations about the physical environment). *Operations* are reactions to these events that modify the structure of the *social participation network*. That is, operations manage *participatory links* among people and digital entities.

Table 1. Social participation network events and operations.

Operations & events	Type	Description
`engagesIn`	event	An actor engages in an action
`showsInterestIn`	event	An actor shows interest for a theme
`create link`	operation	Creates a link between two nodes

3.1   The Network Ontology

We formalize the entities and relations of social participation networks using an ontology. This provides us with a formal foundation to: discover new participatory relationships using inference engines, verify the network consistency, compose Social *Participation* Networks, and build participatory platforms and services by creating instances of the ontology classes.

There already exist ontologies that establish participation concepts. For instance, [10] defines the concepts and relations of traditional participatory scenarios such as persons, organizations, causes and supporters. Another example is [19] that focuses on digital paricipation, thereby addressing the specification of both supporting software platforms and democratic processes and projects.

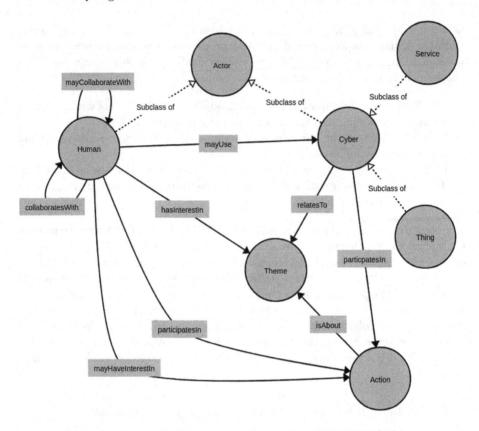

Fig. 2. The network ontology modeled using WebVOWL [27].

Our ontology differs in that it includes not only human participants but also IoT devices and software services, which are essential to the implementation of digital participation.

Figure 2 outlines the social participation network ontology. It is composed of three main classes:

– *Actor*: Actor has the subclasses *Human* and *Cyber*. *Cyber* has two subclasses: *Thing* and *Service*. Things can be connected sensors, actuators and appliances, and also more powerful devices such as mobile phones. Services are cloud services, Web Services, APIs, databases, etc.
– *Theme*: Themes are topics representing subjects of interest such as parks, security and climate change, just to mention some examples.
– *Action*: Actions represent concrete projects aiming at doing something; for example, rethinking a particular park in the city, improving the security of a particular street, or reducing carbon emissions around schools.

In the following, we denote with lowercase letters h, c, t and a, the instances of the classes *Human*, *Cyber*, *Theme* and *Action*, respectively. The ontology also introduces two types of relations:

- *Explicit* relations are defined based on the declared behavior of actors. A base explicit relation is *hasInterestIn* with which a human can relate to a theme. Actions and cybers may also relate to themes through the *isAbout* and *relatesTo* relations. Humans can relate to other humans through the relations *collaboratesWith*, meaning the humans participate in the same action.
- *Implicit* relations characterize inferred relations. They derive from the explicit ones and their labels add the prefix *may* (e.g., *mayHaveInterestIn*) as the relationships are inferred by the system as opposed to being explicitly specified.

3.2 Social Participation Network Invariants and Dynamics

In the last years, several initiatives have emerged to build rule-based systems for the Social IoT where rules automate the formation of social links between IoT devices and allow the inference of new relations. Examples of such systems are diverse (see [22] for a survey) and include, e.g., University & Car Pooling, and Trust Management & Smart Building. In a way similar to these works, this section introduces rules associated with the management of *"participatory links"*, although it focuses only on the case of creation.

We first define the invariant properties of any *Social Participation Network* for which the two following Rules 1 and 2 must always hold.

Rule 1. *Every registered human declares at least one theme of interest:*

$$\forall h \in Human, \ \exists t \in Theme : \ h \xrightarrow{hasInterestIn} t$$

Rule 2. *Every action, thing and service relates to at least one theme:*

$$\forall a \in Action, \ \exists t \in Theme : \ a \xrightarrow{isAbout} t$$
$$\forall c \in Cyber, \ \exists t \in Theme : \ c \xrightarrow{relatesTo} t$$

The dynamics of social participation networks results from the occurrence of events (e.g., see Table 1) as the two next rules specify.

Rule 3. *If a user shows interest in a theme, a link is created between that human and that theme:*

$$\exists h \in Human, \exists t \in Theme : \texttt{showsInterestIn}(h,t) : h \xrightarrow{hasInterestIn} t$$

Furthermore, the link mayUse is created between that human and all the cybers (things and services) related to that theme:

$$\exists h \in Human, \exists t \in Theme, \exists c \in Cyber :$$
$$h \xrightarrow{hasInterestIn} t \wedge c \xrightarrow{relatesTo} t : h \xrightarrow{mayUse} c$$

And, the link mayHaveInterestIn is created between that human and all the actions that relate to that theme:

$$\exists h \in Human, \exists t \in Theme, \exists a \in Action :$$
$$h \xrightarrow{hasInterestIn} t \wedge a \xrightarrow{isAbout} t : h \xrightarrow{mayHaveInterestIn} a$$

Finally, if two humans are interested in the same theme, the link mayCollabo-rateWith is created between them:

$$\exists h_1, \ h_2 \in Human, \exists t \in Theme :$$
$$h_1 \xrightarrow{hasInterestIn} t \wedge h_2 \xrightarrow{hasInterestIn} t : h_1 \xrightarrow{mayCollaborateWith} h_2 \wedge$$
$$h_2 \xrightarrow{mayCollaborateWith} h_1$$

Rule 4. *If a human engages in an action, the link participatesIn is created for that action.*

$$\exists h \in Human, \exists a \in Action : \mathbf{engagesIn}(h, a) : h \xrightarrow{participatesIn} a$$

Following, if two users engage in the same action, then the link collaboratesWith is created between them.

$$\exists h_1, \ h_2 \in Human, \exists a \in Action : h_1 \xrightarrow{participatesIn} a \wedge h_2 \xrightarrow{participatesIn} a :$$
$$h_1 \xrightarrow{collaboratesWith} h_2 \wedge h_2 \xrightarrow{collaboratesWith} h_1$$

The rules we presented in this section are an early formalization of the social participation network paradigm. While the paradigm builds on those of social network and social IoT, it goes further by addressing the necessary connection among people and cyber entities within participatory processes. We are currently analyzing the rich literature on digital participation in order to discover the core set of rules for participation. However, we do not pretend to introduce a fixed set, other rules can be added during the design phase of a participatory process to meet specific needs. In addition, although we have not presented rules associated with the removal of links, they are similar to those presented in this section.

4   Designing an Online Social Network Service for Participation

The *social participation network* paradigm paves the way for the design of an associated *Participatory OSNS* (Online Social Network Service), through which people may connect and collaborate together as well as with relevant cyber-entities to engage in participatory processes. One key feature of the participatory OSNS is to provide interoperability across the heterogeneous cyber entities, including the diverse online communication services people use (from email to popular OSNSes). We have previously introduced the *social middleware* solution to address such interoperability requirements [2]. In particular, social middleware leverages the Universal Social Network Bus [3] which mediates interaction across online communication technologies to overcome the platform lock-in.

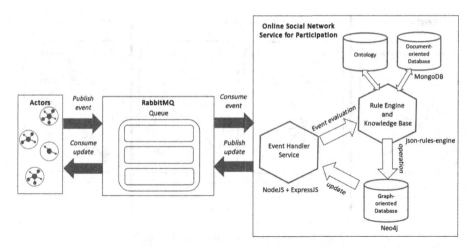

Fig. 3. Participatory OSNS architecture.

Participatory OSNS Architecture: Building on the above contributions and state-of-the-art technology building blocks, Fig. 3 depicts the architecture design of a participatory OSNS. The architecture includes the *Event Handler Service* as a `Node.js` (www.nodejs.org) and `Express` (www.expressjs.com) application. *Actors*, in a given *participatory context*, then trigger events such as *engagesIn* and *showsInterestIn*, which are published to a message broker such as `RabbitMQ` (www.rabbitmq.com) (see *Publish event* in Fig. 3). The *Event Handler Service* consumes events from the message broker (see *Consume event* in Fig. 3), which it evaluates using the *Rule Engine and Knowledge Base* containing the social participation network rules we presented in Sect. 3.2 (see *Event evaluation* in Fig. 3). The rules are stored in a `MongoDB` (www.mongodb.com) database as `Json` documents. If the event evaluation triggers an operation, the social participation network graph structure is updated accordingly (see *operation* in Fig. 3), where we leverage the graph-oriented database `Neo4j` (www.neo4j.com), to store the social participation network graph. Finally, actors receive an updated version of the social participation network graph that concerns them (see *Publish update* and *Consume update* in Fig. 3).

Privacy-Preserving Participation: Participatory technologies such as the proposed dedicated OSNS can support a wide range of activities. However, the possibility of gathering unprecedented amount of information can endanger the privacy of people. This is a threat that participatory technologies share with the more global paradigm of smart cities [18] and, in general, with any online activity [11]. A base requirement is for any participatory service/platform to enforce the isolation of the diverse participation contexts (e.g., consultation within an enterprise, participatory budgeting campaign, neighborhood co-creation initiatives, ...).

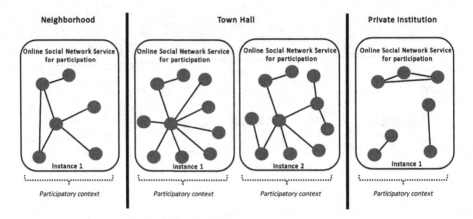

Fig. 4. Participatory process isolation.

Figure 4 illustrates the isolation of participatory processes. The social participation network graph and its associated data hosted by a Town Hall is distinct and isolated from the one hosted by a group of neighbors and by a private institution. The Town Hall hosts two instances for two participatory contexts, which can have different participants and relations among them. The main goal is to protect information such as who are the participants, their personal and private data and their participation contributions. This example shows the two main levels of *participatory process isolation*:

1. *Service provider-level*: The isolation is at the level of the party -or consortium- interested in setting up the participatory process. The interested parties act as *service providers*, as they host an OSNS for the participation instance -or are responsible for finding an appropriate host-.
2. *Participatory context-level*: The isolation is at the level of participants contributions and interactions. All information remains isolated among different participatory contexts even within the same service provider.

5   Conclusions and Future Work

We have introduced and formalized the paradigm of *Social Participation Network* to capture the diverse *participation relationships* – between people, digital services and connected things – supporting *participatory processes*. In a nutshell, the introduced relationships allow automating the finding of: potential collaborators by commonality of interests, participatory actions, and relevant information coming from digital services. We have presented an early formalization of the rules allowing the creation and management of a *Social Participation Network* together with the architecture design of an associated *Participatory Online Social Network Service*. Moreover, we recommend the instantiation of social participation networks within distinct participation contexts—spanning, e.g., private institutions, neighbor communities, and governmental institutions—to protect personal data and privacy given the diverse, and maybe sensitive, participatory contexts.

The work we presented here is preliminary and there are still open questions regarding the conceptualisation and implementation of *Social Participation Networks*. As part of our ongoing and future work, we are developing key technical aspects of our architecture design, such as the integration of heterogeneous IoT devices and software services, as part of the extension of the Universal Social Network Bus [3]. We are also studying the definition of additional social participation network rules to automatically learn and adapt the embedded participatory links. We also plan to evaluate our work both by simulations of participatory contexts and by running small real use cases. Finally, it is crucial to address key challenges facing digital participation, such as the digital divide since not everyone has Internet access and/or is digital literate, and improving the level of engagement by supporting the right participation incentives.

References

1. Aitamurto, T.: Crowdsourcing for democracy: a new era in policy-making. No. 1/2012 in Publication of the Committee for the Future, Parliament of Finland, Helsinki (2012)
2. Angarita, R., Georgantas, N., Issarny, V.: Social middleware for civic engagement. In: 2019 IEEE 39th International Conference on Distributed Computing Systems (ICDCS), pp. 1777–1786. IEEE (2019)
3. Angarita, R., Lefèvre, B., Ahvar, S., Ahvar, E., Georgantas, N., Issarny, V.: Universal social network bus. ACM Trans. Internet Technol. **9**(4), 21
4. Arnstein, S.R.: A ladder of citizen participation. J. Am. Inst. Planners **35**(4), 216–224 (1969)
5. Atzori, L., Iera, A., Morabito, G., Nitti, M.: The Social Internet of Things (SIoT)-when social networks meet the Internet of Things: concept, architecture and network characterization. Comput. Netw. **56**(16), 3594–3608 (2012)
6. Caldeira, T., Holston, J.: Participatory urban planning in Brazil. Urban Stud. **52**(11), 2001–2017 (2015)
7. Chan, C.M.: From open data to open innovation strategies: creating e-services using open government data. In: 2013 46th Hawaii International Conference on System Sciences, pp. 1890–1899. IEEE (2013)
8. Christensen, H.S., Karjalainen, M., Nurminen, L.: Does crowdsourcing legislation increase political legitimacy? The case of avoin ministeriö in Finland. Policy Internet **7**(1), 25–45 (2015)
9. Crivellaro, C., Comber, R., Bowers, J., Wright, P.C., Olivier, P.: A pool of dreams: Facebook, politics and the emergence of a social movement. In: Proceedings of the 32nd Annual ACM Conference on Human Factors in Computing Systems - CHI 2014, pp. 3573–3582. ACM Press, Toronto (2014)
10. Fabbri, R., Filho, H.P.P., de Luna, R.B., Martins, R.A.P., Amanqui, F.K.M., de Abreu Moreira, D.: Social participation ontology: community documentation, enhancements and use examples. CoRR abs/1501.02662 (2015)
11. Fernández, D.: Where is online privacy going? Glob. Priv. Law Rev. **1**(1), 55–60 (2020)

12. Halpern, D., Gibbs, J.: Social media as a catalyst for online deliberation? Exploring the affordances of Facebook and YouTube for political expression. Comput. Hum. Behav. **29**(3), 1159–1168 (2013)
13. Hansson, K., Belkacem, K., Ekenberg, L.: Open government and democracy: a research review. Soc. Sci. Comput. Rev. **33**(5), 540–555 (2015)
14. Hellström, J.: Crowdsourcing development: from funding to reporting, pp. 635–647. Palgrave Macmillan UK, London (2016)
15. Holston, J., Issarny, V., Parra, C.: Engineering software assemblies for participatory democracy: the participatory budgeting use case. In: Software Engineering in Society at ICSE, Austin, TX, United States, May 2016
16. Kalampokis, E., Tambouris, E., Tarabanis, K.: Open government data: a stage model. In: Janssen, M., Scholl, H.J., Wimmer, M.A., Tan, Y. (eds.) EGOV 2011. LNCS, vol. 6846, pp. 235–246. Springer, Heidelberg (2011). https://doi.org/10.1007/978-3-642-22878-0_20
17. Landemore, H.: Inclusive constitution-making: the icelandic experiment. J. Polit. Philos. **23**(2), 166–191 (2015)
18. Martínez-Ballesté, A., Pérez-Martínez, P.A., Solanas, A.: The pursuit of citizens' privacy: a privacy-aware smart city is possible. IEEE Commun. Mag. **51**(6), 136–141 (2013)
19. Porwol, L., Ojo, A., Breslin, J.G.: An ontology for next generation e-participation initiatives. Gov. Inf. Q. **33**(3), 583–594 (2016)
20. Qanbari, S., Rekabsaz, N., Dustdar, S.: Open government data as a service (GoDaaS): big data platform for mobile app developers. In: 2015 3rd International Conference on Future Internet of Things and Cloud, pp. 398–403. IEEE, Rome, August 2015
21. Quittkat, C.: The European commission's online consultations: a success story? JCMS: J. Common Market Stud. **49**(3), 653–674 (2011)
22. Roopa, M., Pattar, S., Buyya, R., Venugopal, K.R., Iyengar, S., Patnaik, L.: Social Internet of Things (SIoT): foundations, thrust areas, systematic review and future directions. Comput. Commun. **139**, 32–57 (2019)
23. Salim, F., Haque, U.: Urban computing in the wild: a survey on large scale participation and citizen engagement with ubiquitous computing, cyber physical systems, and Internet of Things. Int. J. Hum. Comput. Stud. **81**, 31–48 (2015)
24. Seifert, A., Rössel, J.: Digital participation. In: Gu, D., Dupre, M. (eds.) Encyclopedia of Gerontology and Population Aging, pp. 1–5. Springer, Cham (2019). https://doi.org/10.1007/978-3-319-69892-2_1017-1
25. Ubaldi, B.: Open government data (2013)
26. Wang, C.Y., Yang, H.Y., Seng-cho, T.C.: Using peer-to-peer technology for knowledge sharing in communities of practices. Decis. Support Syst. **45**(3), 528–540 (2008)
27. Wiens, V., Lohmann, S., Auer, S.: WebVOWL editor: device-independent visual ontology modeling. In: International Semantic Web Conference (P&D/Industry/BlueSky) (2018)
28. Zheng, Y., Capra, L., Wolfson, O., Yang, H.: Urban computing: concepts, methodologies, and applications. ACM Trans. Intell. Syst. Technol. **5**(3), 1–55 (2014)

EcoSoft: Proposition of an Eco-Label for Software Sustainability

Rébecca Deneckère[✉] and Gregoria Rubio

Centre de Recherche en Informatique, University Paris 1 Panthéon-Sorbonne,
Paris, France
Rebecca.deneckere@univ-parisl.fr

Abstract. There is an increasing interest in corporate sustainability and how companies should include it to satisfy user's requirements concerning social, economic, and environmental impacts. Research about sustainability in computer science aims to offer methods, techniques and tools to lessen the impact of new technologies on the environment, to offer a better world, a smarter life, to the next generations. Information systems must participate in the collective effort to move towards sustainable development, and software and application companies must lead a CSR strategy to achieve this aim. Moreover, beyond an individual company approach, sustainability should be seen as an integral quality of any software (as well as safety, performance or reliability). All of this seem obvious at a time when applications and programs of all kinds are ubiquitous in everyday life. Nevertheless, the challenges of sustainable development have still not been considered in certain key sectors such as the development of information technology. A lot of ecolabels exist for a lot of different products, although not for software sustainability. We propose in this work an ecolabel for software sustainability, based on a set of relevant criteria found in different works.

Keywords: Sustainability · Ecolabel · Software

1 Introduction

The 21st century is a period of new technologies and could be called the digital age. It is also a period that is very affected by sustainable development issues that apply to all aspects of our society. Information technologies, because of their importance, do not escape preoccupations and questions as to their role and responsibility in developing a more respectful and sustainable economic model. As defined for the first time in 1987 in the Brundtland Report, «humanity has the ability to make development sustainable to ensure that it meets the needs of the present without compromising the ability of future generations to meet their own needs [1]. This involves a gradual transformation of the economy and society across the spectrum of sustainability.

As a result, international communities have become aware of the need to control greenhouse gas emissions, which are the main drivers of climate change, and therefore to reduce energy consumption and carbon footprint globally [2]. In this context, information technologies have an ambivalent role: they reduce the impact on the

S. Dupuy-Chessa and H. A. Proper (Eds.): CAiSE 2020 Workshops, LNBIP 382, pp. 121–132, 2020.
https://doi.org/10.1007/978-3-030-49165-9_11

environment in certain contexts of use, notably through virtualization or business process optimization. However, in other cases they are themselves responsible for negative effects on the environment, such as the very energy-intensive use of data centers [3]. This global dematerialization continues, particularly with the transition to the cloud, making IT responsible for 10% of global electricity consumption in 2017 [4]. Information technology must therefore be fully considered in sustainable development actions and more particularly in companies social and environmental responsibility (CSR) strategies. It is therefore essential to be able to provide models, methods and tools which allow, first, to measure and assess the impact of technologies on the environment, and then, second, to be able to apply tools in the development process of these technologies in order to improve their sustainability.

Research on information technology and computer science in general aims to make technologies more efficient and efficient, to create a smarter planet [5]. In this new business model, the sustainability aspect is more rarely considered. Sustainable development efforts in the information technology sector have so far focused on infrastructure (data centers) and the manufacturing of hardware [6]. The data centers are particularly targeted by the objectives of reducing energy consumption in the IT sector, considering both their importance in the infrastructure of enterprises and their data, and their considerable energy requirements. In 2012, the European Union even took the lead by launching a project called GAMES (Green Active Management of Energy in IT Service centers), which aims to develop a set of tools, methods and techniques for managing the energy performance of next-generation data centers [7]. For both data centers and other information technology infrastructure and services, the source of energy consumption is in the software layer [8]. As a result, a reduction in the resource consumption of software components leads to a reduction in the electricity consumption of computer equipment. The software layer is therefore an important if not crucial lever in reducing ICT energy consumption.

Since 2010, there has been growing interest in research on the concept of sustainability in computer engineering, but sustainable development applied to information technology remains a less important topic [9]. Nevertheless, the ever-increasing number of scientific publications on the subject shows that researchers are interested in defining and developing concepts for sustainability in software engineering. This includes characterizing models, methods and tools to reduce the life cycle impact of software products and their development.

The definition of sustainability in software engineering brings together several possible characterizations but we will retain the following one for the continuation of this work. "Sustainable Software is software, whose impacts on economy, society, human beings, and environment that result from development, deployment, and usage of the software are minimal and/or which have a positive effect on sustainable development." [10].

In this paper, we will focus on the environmental sustainability framework. The impact of new technologies on the environment is rather ambiguous because, as stated earlier, they can be both a benefit and a harm. For a more in-depth analysis of their impact, it is also necessary to consider the different phases of their life cycle and the effects associated with them: the effects due to the production of information technology, effects due to their use and systemic effects.

- Production effects consider the use and consumption of natural resources, as well as pollution associated with the extraction of raw materials and end-of-life electronic waste.
- The effects of use concern the positive indirect effects of their use, such as process optimization and product virtualization and simulation, and thus the conservation of natural resources.
- The systemic effects concern the long-term indirect effects resulting from the use of information technology, such as changing lifestyles that encourage stronger economic growth leading to a rebound effect as resource consumption increases.

These effects on the environment, in order to be controlled, must be measured and evaluated and therefore monitored by companies. It is the commitment of these companies to contribute to the sustainable development of their information systems and technologies that is crucial.

Companies and organizations, by their place in society, have social responsibility for their practices and the effects they have on society [11]. Their activities and decisions directly influence the economy, making their commitment to sustainable development all the more important in reducing the digital environmental footprint. To help and encourage companies to become more involved in social responsibility, ISO 26000 was created in 2014 to provide guidelines for the implementation of sustainable practices. Sustainability is approached in a multidimensional way around 7 areas of action: communities and local development, human rights, relations and working conditions, consumer issues, the loyalty of practices and the environment. On the occasion of the Horizon 2020 program for research and innovation, the European Commission has also launched a platform providing information technology companies with a set of tools and methodologies to assess the energy consumption and the carbon footprint associated with technologies they use and develop[1]. This initiative aims to encourage companies to move towards eco-design by developing software solutions that use fewer resources and have a longer lifespan. Companies, in particular software publishers, must be responsible for the management of their information systems and the programs they sell to their customers.

The sustainable development strategy for companies is increasingly an important competitive advantage for their growth, particularly because of the influence it has on their brand image. In addition to financial gains, such as reducing energy bills, this gives them an image of responsibility that is increasingly important for consumers. The benefits of a sustainability policy convince an increasing number of structures to integrate CSR objectives into their business models [12]. In particular, new technology companies are a real lever for reducing the consumption of energy resources, and even more for reducing the environmental impacts of ICT [13].

So, the problem today is the lack of clear consensus and definitions about sustainability in software engineering. In order to move towards sustainable development, information systems must participate in the collective effort and software and application companies must pursue a CSR strategy geared to the sustainability of software development. So how can sustainability be integrated into software development?

---

[1] https://ictfootprint.eu/.

More specifically, how can ecodesign be integrated into software and application development?

We will be looking at the concept of software eco-design as a way to make the software layer of new technologies more environmentally friendly. It will be a question of how digital players, whether government, organizations, businesses or users, can make software and applications more sustainable, particularly in terms of energy efficiency.

This work will first look at the related works in the field of ecolabeling. Then, the proposed EcoSoft label is presented with all the defined criteria in Sect. 2. We conclude in Sect. 3.

2 Related Works

More and more consumers are considering the ecological dimension of the products they buy and use in line with the growing interest in environmental issues [13]. Eco-labels were then introduced to meet this demand, with more than 450 consumer labels worldwide awarded by governments, organizations or consumer associations in 2016 [14]. These labels help consumers to identify more responsible products and to choose according to criteria that integrate environmental quality. Labels, especially if assigned by official authorities, are a guarantee of consumer confidence and credibility [15].

An eco-label is a quality label that certifies that a product or service has a reduced impact on the environment. It aims to "promote the design, production, marketing and use of products with less impact on the environment throughout their life cycle" and "better inform consumers of the effects of products on the environment, without compromising the safety of the product or workers, or significantly affecting the qualities that make the product suitable for use"[2].

An eco-label may certify products and services of different categories which comply with certain ecological criteria. For example, we find labels for food (Organic Agriculture label), textile (GOTS label[3]), tourist accommodation (Panda Gîte label[4]), electronic devices (Energy Star label[5]), wood (FSC label[6]) or cosmetics (label Cosmebio[7]).

The award of an eco-label is usually based on a balance record and a life cycle analysis of the product carried out by a national or international public entity, or delegated to an independent accredited entity. It may be evidenced by a distinguishing sign such as a pictogram on the product, a label or a name in order to be easily identified by the public and consumers.

---

[2] http://www.ecolabels.fr/fr/espace-consommateurs/les-ecolabels.

[3] https://www.global-standard.org/fr/.

[4] https://ecotourisme.gites-de-france.com/notre-demarche-panda.html.

[5] https://www.energystar.gov/.

[6] https://fr.fsc.org/fr-fr.

[7] https://www.cosmebio.org/en/.

There are a multitude of labels related to ICT products. The multiplicity of products and the complexity of production chains make it difficult to create a single label. Labels are classified according to their type, that is to say to which organization they come from, by which standards they are regulated. There are currently three different types of labels that can attest to the ability of products to comply with a sustainability approach by certifying that the environmental impacts of the labelled products are low compared to those of other products on the market.

Type 1 brings together official labels, that is to say they are proposed by local authorities (state, European Union), public interest groups (AFNOR – the French standards association, for example) or self-reported by an ONG. These labels under ISO 14024 meet strict specifications and their certification is regularly reviewed by independent certifiers. They consider the entire product life cycle (LCA approach). The best-known type 1 ecolabels are the European ecolabel, the NF French environment label, the Blue Angel of German origin (focuses on health, climate, water, and resources) and the International Energy Star, for the energy efficiency of products. The TCO label adds a humanitarian aspect to the environmental aspect since it certifies the creation of products minimizing the impact on human health.

The self-declarations correspond to the Type 2 eco-labels. They fall under ISO 14021 and are developed under the responsibility of companies alone. In general, they concern only part of a product's life cycle or relate to a single environmental characteristic of the product. The associated standard frames self-declarations by specific criteria: it must not be misleading, be clearly presented, be verifiable, etc. The best known is the EPEAT label created in the United States by the Green electronic Council which allows companies to evaluate IT equipment according to their eco-characteristics. This label is now used worldwide by a large number of companies. The ECMA-370 standard provides a system of measures and environmental features to help companies in the ICT sector in the creation of self-declarations.

Ecoprofiles are type 3 eco-labels, covered by ISO 14025. Their allocation is the result of a LCA and allows a comparison between products of the same category at the level of resource consumption, greenhouse gas emissions, and waste.

In the field of new technologies, labelling is difficult to achieve because of the virtual dimension of products (software, applications, websites) which makes users believe that they have no impact on the environment. It is therefore important to add value to software that is developed in a sustainable way, and labeling is a way to give them more visibility. By engaging in the implementation of digital technology certifications and labels, governments, particularly at European and global levels, would help legitimise software eco-design in the eyes of users. Companies that make the effort to achieve a sustainable strategy in the development of their products also gain credibility compared to their competitors when this approach is formally recognized [16]. A sustainability label for digital software and services such as EcoSoft would therefore serve this objective of bringing more visibility and therefore credibility to ecodesign in the software field. [17] proposes a discussion about the labelisation of sustainable software products and websites and list a set of possible criteria that can be applied by separating them in different types. Criteria for green web content management systems and web applications can be found in [18].

3   EcoSoft, an Eco-Label for Software Sustainability

We propose the establishment of a sustainability label for software that would allow users to choose programs and applications based on their impact on the environment. This label would be a way for consumers to easily identify the most durable software and thus be able to limit their carbon use as users. It is also an approach that helps to make the company aware of the environmental impacts of digital software and services and to be able to implement a commitment to sustainable development. The company reduces its software footprint and at the same time promotes its image through this eco-design approach.

Like the Energy Star label on energy-efficient electronic devices, the EcoSoft label would serve to inform about the voluntary commitment made by designers on the energy efficiency of software on a computer, a tablet or smartphone according to several criteria. It would be valid for a period of 2 years, maximum duration given the many developments and updates that occur in the life of a software or application. The software or web application would be given a distinctive logo to make its certification visible. There is a similar project for eco-design of websites in particular called Green Code Label[8] which labels websites developed according to web design methods. However, there is no European or international label that certifies the sustainability of an application service. Indeed, the official eco-label of the European Union[9] does not certify digital products and services, which would make the EcoSoft label a reference in the field of sustainable software certification.

A software labeled EcoSoft must meet sustainability criteria. It must have been developed in accordance with software ecodesign techniques by integrating the tools and methods of sustainable management of the complete product life cycle. EcoSoft is a multi-criteria label, that is to say that its awarding is based on the respect of a set of predefined criteria, and therefore it could not be granted on the basis of a single criterion. Digital softwares, applications and services of all categories and types can be certified. There are also no restrictions on the source of the program.

Following the Greensoft model [19], a software can be analyzed according to the three phases of its life cycle: the development phase, the usage phase, the end-of-life phase. Our EcoSoft label will use criteria than can be classified following these three phases, as shown in Table 1. However, on the contrary of the Greensoft model, our eco-label will only specifically address criteria concerning software. It will not take into account the criteria relating to the energy consumption of computers and other hardware machines, as well as the energy required for the company's infrastructure. In this work, we have choose criteria into the two facets of sustainability defined by [20]: the sustainability BY the software (ICT4Green) and the sustainability IN the software (GreenIT).

---

[8] https://label.greencodelab.org/.

[9] Site officiel écolabel européen: http://ec.europa.eu/environment/ecolabel/eu-ecolabel-products-and-services.html.

Table 1. EcoSoft criteria.

Development phase	
Sustainable documents	Download size
Sustainable specification	Hardware requirements
Code optimization	Green analysis efficiency
Usage phase	
Accessibility	Material resource consumption
Usability	Backup size
Energy efficiency at running time	
End of life phase	
Data conversion to the future	Long-term data storage
Software or application	Packaging and manuals

This section presents all the criteria listed in Table 1. Each criteria is described with two possible values, the first one indicates that efforts have been done to obtain a sustainable software, although the second one indicates the contrary. The awarding of the label should mean that all criteria of the list are respected.

3.1   Development Phase

The criteria for the conception and design phase are the following.

Sustainable documents {up-to-date and integrating sustainable techniques; outdated or not sustainable}
The creation and/or provision of reference documents in ecodesign to stakeholders have to be taken into account. This criterion comes before the start of the project. In the design phase, it is a question of being able to provide project stakeholders with reference material enabling them to integrate sustainable design techniques in the form of good practices, recommendations, checklists, examples of implementation, etc. It also take into account the maintainability of the software in order to analyse and change files in an effective and efficient way, regarding the source code but also the content [17]. This relates also to the modifiability criteria proposed in [21].

Sustainable specification {eco-designed specifications; no good practice application}
The software ecodesign is also based on a specification writing directed towards sustainability with precise functional specifications without unnecessary functionalities and without unnecessary data production [22]. The expression of adapted functional needs determines the quality of the software and in particular its efficiency. Indeed, every feature of the program consumes CPU and memory resources during use even if they are in the background [22]. The preliminary draft of the specifications should then include the drafting of a complete specification consisting of functional and technical specifications that comply with ecodesign standards, including clear modelling of the

program [19], for instance by using clear and precise UML specifications. As said in [23] a new form of requirements 'Environment Requirements' need to be added to the non functional usual requirements.

Code optimization {optimized; not optimized}

Programming of the software must be carried out in accordance with good ecodesign practices. Software ecodesign focuses on functional, graphic, ergonomic and technical design. In case of a software, we recommend that at least 2/3 of the techniques provided by the software ecodesign referential (in constant evolution)[10] should have been applied in order to value the criteria as 'optimized'. We propose to use a checklist to identify the used techniques. In case of an application, we recommend that at least 65 of the 115 best practices proposed [24] have been applied in order to value the criteria as 'optimized'. We propose to use the Opquast checklist[11] to work.

Download size {optimized; not optimized}

More and more software products are nowadays downloadable. We recommend that the size of the downloaded software should be optimized to the maximum [19]. Many techniques exist to reduce download size so they should be used to do it.

Hardware requirements {average configuration; powerful configuration}

End-user influence is high as nearly 90% of the energy used by ICT hardware can be attributed to the application software running on it [25]. As a result, it is necessary to maximize the hardware lifetime by its actual physical durability rather than forcing its obsolescenc by software platform requirements [21]. If the requirements needs too powerful hardware, it will induce the buying of new material to be able to run the software. It then must be able to operate with hardware that is at an average configuration compared to current standards to avoid replacement and new hardware purchases [19, 26]. This can be related to the Portability criteria of [21].

Green analysis efficiency

[27] proposes to add a green analysis stage to promote energy efficiency. It determines the greenness of each increment of the system that is developing. This stage acts like a testing stage but for energy efficiency. Metrics are used is this stage to perform the analysis (CPU usage, Green Performance Indicators, etc.).

3.2   Usage Phase

The criteria used for the usage phase are the following.

Accessibility {improved; not improved}

Software ecodesign also addresses the social dimension such as digital accessibility. Good development practices improve the user experience, especially for people with disabilities. For people with colour blindness, for example, graphs cannot be understood if colours cannot be identified. The software or application should then be

---

[10] Software ecodesign referential: https://collab.greencodelab.org/.

[11] https://checklists.opquast.com/fr/eco-conception/.

designed to comply with good accessibility practices to enable navigation for all audiences. We recommend to use the standards of W3C[12].

Usability {optimized, not optimized}

The software or application should be user-friendly [21]. If the customer satisfaction if high, the support cost is low. We recommend to use 2/3 of the usability guidelines proposed by [28].

Energy efficiency at running time {optimized; not optimized}

[29] states that efficiency defines how software behaves when it comes to saving resources. We recommend that the program must not have an eco-score of less than 70/100 on the Greenspector test[13] in order for the criteria to obtain the value «optimized» . This can be related to the performance criteria of [21].

Material resource consumption {optimized; not optimized}

It is important to identify the resource consumption of the various components of the software. In [30], the authors distinguish a set of software components to be analyzed in terms of energy consumption. For example, there is the software architecture, RAM, processor (also called CPU), storage or source code to take into account. For these energy consumption measurements, the code must be analysed with diagnostic tools to determine whether the ecodesign methods have been complied with, for instance PowerAPI [31], Greenspector[14], Intel SoC Watch[15], Chisel [32]. We recommend to use Greenspector and to obtain an eco score of more than 70/100 to the test (CPU, memory, mAh deload) for classifying the criteria as «optimized».

Backup size {optimized; not optimized}

It is possible to optimize the energy consumption necessary for the backup of software data or application over the long term. Reducing the number of backups can also be a possible optimization. By eliminating the problem of constantly backing up the same copy of a file again and again, data de-duplication can decrease backup storage consumption by 10 to 50 times compared to traditional tape-based backup methods. Since less data is sent across the infrastructure, data de-duplication also can reduce the bandwidth consumed by traditional network-based backups by up to 500 times [34].

3.3   End-of-Life Phase

The criteria used for the end-of-life phase are the following.

Data conversion to the future {OpenSource format; Proprietary format}

The data of the current program must be of a format allowing easy transfer to the future software (essentially open source formats), otherwise data can causes compatibility issues and energy and material resource consumption issues [19].

---

[12] https://www.w3.org/WAI/.

[13] https://greenspector.com/fr/product/.

[14] https://greenspector.com/fr/.

[15] https://software.intel.com/en-us/socwatch-help-energy-analysis-workflows.

Long-term data storage (back-up) {optimized, not optimized}
The energy consumption needed to back up software data or long-term application should be optimized [19]. Sometimes, legal regulations require long-term storage data and the backup storage size will increase.

Packaging and manuals {recyclable; not recyclable}
If the software or application contains a packaging and/or user manuals in paper form, these documents must be recycled [19].

4 Conclusion

The label we propose here is at the theoretical stage and has not yet been tested on practical cases. EcoSoft is an eco-label that takes into account the involvement of stakeholders (project manager, software architects, developers) in the process of integrating sustainability into the project. The three stages of the software's life cycle, namely the development, usage and end of life, are analyzed to determine the environmental impacts they generate. We focused the analysis on the energy consumption of software components, which is an important aspect for the overall quality of the software, especially for the user experience on the mobile device, but also because digital energy consumption has a high environmental footprint.

The field of software and its technologies is constantly evolving, especially in the forms that the software can take. In this sense, the label could evolve by adapting the criteria to the type of software analyzed in order to be able to take into account its specificities (application software, web applications, system software...).

Our future work will be to validate the chosen criteria with a set of professionals. Then to test these criteria on several softwares in order to define if they can be awarded the label EcoSoft.

References

1. Brundtland, B., Khalid, M., Agnelli, S.: Report of the World Commission on Environment and Development: Our Common Future ('Brundtland report'). World Commission on Environment and Development. Tokyo, Japan (1987)
2. Unfccc.int. The Paris Agreement - main page. http://unfccc.int/paris_agreement/items/9485. php. Accessed June 2018
3. Breuil, H., Burette, D., Flüry-Hérard, B., Cueugniet, J., Vignolles, D.: Rapport TIC et Développement durable. Ministère de l'écologie, de l'énergie, du développement durable et de l'aménagement du territoire (MEEDDAT), p. 96 (2008)
4. Cailloce, L.: Numérique: le grand gâchis énergétique. CNRS Le J. (2018). https://lejournal. cnrs.fr/articles/numerique-le-grand-gachis-energetique
5. Lenssen, G.G., Smith, N.C.: IBM and Sustainability: Creating a Smarter Planet, In: Lenssen, G., Smith, N. (eds.) Managing Sustainable Business, pp. 549–556. Springer, Heidelberg (2018). https://doi.org/10.1007/978-94-024-1144-7_25
6. Hilty, L., Aebischer, B.: ICT Innovations for Sustainability. Springer, Heidelberg (2015). https://doi.org/10.1007/978-3-319-09228-7

7. Pernici, B., et al.: Setting energy efficiency goals in data centres: the GAMES approach. In: Huusko, J., de Meer, H., Klingert, S., Somov, A. (eds.) E2DC 2012. LNCS, vol. 7396, pp. 1–12. Springer, Heidelberg (2012). https://doi.org/10.1007/978-3-642-33645-4_1
8. Noureddine, A.: Towards a Better Understanding of the Energy. Thesis of the Lille university (2014)
9. Penzenstadler, B., Bauer, V., Calero, C., Franch, X.: Sustainability in software engineering: a systematic literature review. In: Evaluation & Assessment in Software Engineering (EASE 2012), pp. 32–41 (2012)
10. Dick, M., Naumann, S., Kuhn, N.: A model and selected instances of green and sustainable software. In: Berleur, J., Hercheui, M.D., Hilty, L.M. (eds.) HCC 2010, CIP 2010, vol. 328, pp. 248–259. Springer, Heidelberg (2010). https://doi.org/10.1007/978-3-642-15479-9_24
11. Commission des Communautés Européennes. Livre Vert. Promouvoir un cadre européen pour la responsabilité sociale des entreprises (2001)
12. Watson, R., Boudreau, M., Chen, A.: Information systems and environmentally sustainable development: energy informatics and new directions for the IS community. MIS Q. **34**(1), 23–38 (2010)
13. Eurobarometer. Attitudes of European citizens towards the environment, Special Eurobarometer (2014). http://ec.europa.eu/public_opinion/archives/ebs/ebs_416_en.pdf
14. Ecolabel Index. All Ecolabels (2016). http://www.ecolabelindex.com/ecolabels/
15. Darnall, N., Ji, H., Vazquez-Brust, D.: Third-party certification, sponsorship, and consumers' ecolabel use. J. Bus. Ethics **150**(4), 953–969 (2016)
16. Darnall, N., Aragon-Correa, J.A.: Can ecolabels influence firms sustainability strategy and stakeholder behaviors? Organ. Environ. **27**(4), 319–327 (2014)
17. Kern, E., Dick, M., Naumann, S., Filler, A.: Labelling sustainable software products and websites: ideas, approaches, and challenges. In: 29th International Conference on Informatics for Environmental Protection (EnviroInfo) Third International Conference on ICT for Sustainability (ICT4S) (2015)
18. Dick, M., Kern, E., Johann, T., Naumann, S., Gülden, C.: Green web engineering - measurements and findings. In: 26th International Conference on Informatics on Informatics - Informatics for Environmental Protection, Sustainable Development and Risk Management (EnviroInfo); Federal Environment Agency, Dessau (2012)
19. Naumann, S., Dick, M., Kern, E., Johann, T.: The GREENSOFT model: a reference model for green and sustainable software and its engineering. Sustain. Comput.: Inform. Syst. **1**(4), 294–304 (2011)
20. Calero, C., Piattini, M.: Green in Software Engineering. Springer, Heidelberg (2015). https://doi.org/10.1007/978-3-319-08581-4
21. Albertao, F., Xiao, J., Tian, C., Lu, Y., Zhang, K.Q., Liu, C.: Measuring the sustainability performance of software projects. In: 7th International Conference on e-Business Engineering (ICEBE), Shanghai, China, pp. 369–373 (2010)
22. Vautier, V., Philippot, O.: Is "software eco-design" a solution to reduce the environmental. Electronics Goes Green 2016 + . Berlin (2016)
23. Agarwal, S., Nath, A., Chowdhury, D.: Sustainable approaches and good practices in green software engineering. IJRRCS **3**, 1425–1428 (2012)
24. Bordage, F.: Eco-conception web: les 115 bonnes pratiques, 2e édition, Eyrolles (2015)
25. GeSI. Global e-Sustainability Initiative; wbcsd; World Resource Institute; Carbon Trust. GHG Protocol Product Life Cycle Accounting and Reporting Standard ICT Sector Guidance. Chapter 7 (2013)
26. Hilty, L.M.: Information technology and sustainability. In: Essays on the Relationship between ICT and Sustainable Development, Books on Demand, Norderstedt (2008)

27. Mahmoud, S., Ahmad, I.: A green model for sustainable software engineering. Int. J. Softw. Eng. Appl. **7**(4) (2013)
28. Nielsen, J.: 113 Design Guidelines for Homepage Usability (2001). https://www.nngroup.com/articles/113-design-guidelines-homepage-usability/
29. Taina, J.: Good, bad, and beautiful software - in search of green software quality factors. CEPIS UPGRADE **XII**(4), 22–27 (2011)
30. Lago, P., Gu, Q., Bozzelli, P.: A systematic literature review of green software metrics. VU Technical Report (2014)
31. Noureddine, A., Bourdon, A., Rouvoy, R., Seinturier, L.: A preliminary study of the impact of software engineering on GreenIT. In: International Workshop on Green and Sustainable Software (GREENS), Zurich, Switzerland, pp. 21–27 (2012)
32. Misailovic, S., Carbin, M., Achour, S., Qi, Z., Rinard, M.: Chisel: reliability- and accuracy-aware optimization of approximate computational kernels. In: OOPSLA 2014, Portland (2014)

An Exploratory Approach for Governance of Society for Smarter Life

Michel Léonard[1,2(✉)] and Anastasiya Yurchyshyna[2]

[1] University of Geneva, CUI, route de Drize, 7, Carouge, Geneva, Switzerland
michel.leonard@unige.ch
[2] CINTCOM, Chemin Champ-Claude, 10, Vernier, Switzerland

Abstract. This paper presents an exploratory approach for the governance of Society in the context of Smarter Life. By answering the challenges of the era of Digitalisation, facing profound societal changes, benefiting from multiple innovations, information systems and services play an outstanding role in improving and enhancing life of humans and contribute to the progress in Smarter Life. This exploratory approach is based on information, whilst information systems and services contribute to developing new practices, creating new situations, generating new added value. In this perspective, information and knowledge can be viewed as information common good, which is in the heart of service design. It is essential that services are designed in an exploratory way, by involving multidisciplinary, multi-institutional, even multi-national actors, whose active participation would lead to the development of new value-added services. This can be done thanks to a protected place adapted to co-construction of information services, Tiers-Lieu for Services (TLS). To assist the dynamics of the servitised Society and support its governing in a sustainable way, an institutional instrument, called people-public-private-partnerships for services (4PS), is presented.

Keywords: Governance of Society · Exploratory approach · Tiers-Lieu for Services · 4PS

1 Era of Smarter Life

Our Society lives in a real era of digitalisation, with new technologies enhancing profound transformations in exchanges between people and institutions, changing practices, creating new situations. Whilst it is essential to continually maintain the technological growth and the cognitive unity of the progression of Society, this should also be a safe operating space for Humanity. Furthermore, there are a lot of disseminated initiatives, which propose a lot of services for Smarter Life. To maintain the global sustainability and resilience, a new paradigm is thus required, which would allow integrating the continued development of human societies and the maintenance of the Earth system [1].

It is an urgent task to create the conditions needed to place digitalisation at the service of sustainable development [2]. They address different perspectives. In short term, the advances in digitalisation support and ease sustainability objectives with a

© Springer Nature Switzerland AG 2020
S. Dupuy-Chessa and H. A. Proper (Eds.): CAiSE 2020 Workshops, LNBIP 382, pp. 133–138, 2020.
https://doi.org/10.1007/978-3-030-49165-9_12

view to harmonise digitalisation with the global sustainability goals agreed in 2015 [3]. Sustainable digitalised societies are subjects of medium term. Already today, precautions must be taken to deal with inevitable societal changes that will accompany digitalisation: e.g. radical structural change on the labour markets as a result of advancing automation, networking, creating new activities and jobs, co-design and sharing common goods, to mention just a few. In a long term, the focus is made on the future: the way humans interact with technologies and, more generally, the Information World; risks and challenges to human personality and integrity, ethical aspects of digitalisation, etc. This includes the exploration of the emerging concepts in the innovative area of sustainability and digital technology [4], the results of societal transformations, as well as creation of new practices in governing Society.

This paper is structured as follows. Section 2 discusses the current slants for governing Society and introduces the exploratory approach. Section 3 presents collaborative service design enabled by Tiers-Lieu for Services (TLS). Section 4 describes an institutional instrument, called people-public-private-partnerships for services (4PS).

2   Exploratory Approach for Governing Society

In broad outline, the existing approaches for governing Society in the context of Smarter Life can be described by two slants.

In "top-down" approach, the decisions on governing Society are made by a relatively small group of decision-makers, who belong to steering or executive committees, according to predefined rules (in form of laws, regulations, industrial standards and conceptualized procedures), and imposed on all members of Society. The main advantage of this approach is to encourage consistent studies in comprehending well-developed subjects to implement profoundly-studied strategies (as, for example, in the case of sustainable development goals [5]). At the same time, a risk of the non-inclusiveness of members of Society and different degrees of non-transparency of decision-making governing processes are among its limitations.

"Bottom-up" approach takes into account the successful practices, already efficiently implemented in specific circumstances and domains, by talented persons by means of services. Its advantages concern better identification of risks, broader collaborative knowledge base and agility in making decisions in concrete situations, but they cannot guarantee their applicability and/or consistency in the scope of whole Society.

It becomes obvious that despite the advantages of each of these slants, none of them can address the complexity of governing Society in the context of Smarter Life. A new form of inclusive governance is thus required. Such inclusive governance includes new modes of governance, integrates various practices, performs interdisciplinary analysis covering legal, policy-making and theoretical concerns, develops methods for coordination (e.g. the Open Method of coordination as a technique of EU governance [6]).

In this perspective, we suggest an exploratory approach for governing Society for Smarter Life. Its main idea is as follows. We should not think purely in terms of technologies. We should think in terms of information, information systems and services. We should think in accordance to propulsors in the context of the progression of

Society, and the added value these propulsors are inducing. A propulsor can be a new law, a political or strategic will, a new technology like a digital system, etc. The propulsions of Society are enabled by propulsors into activities of Society in the form of information services. An information service contains a value proposition [7]. Its aim is not limited to increasing the efficiency of existing business processes, but generating additional value for businesses by creating and enabling situations, in which value may emerge.

Information common goods are formed from information services, in order to establish bases of the progression of Society by means of services. They are based on the concept of common goods [8] whose basic resource is of natural origin (pastures and forests). In contrast, the basic resource of the information common goods is artificial: data, information or knowledge. For both natural and information common goods, there is a risk of falling into a tragedy of the commons [9], when unlimited usage (for natural ones) and uncontrolled rush for digital innovations (for information common goods) might lead to their exhaustion. To avoid the tragedy of the commons and make information common goods efficient and resilient, they are organised in an institutional form of informational common. Myriads of services, which are envisaged as information common goods, currently are, have been and will be developing practices, create new situations, lead to new added value. And this added value in services comes from enabling informational commons [10].

The exploratory approach for governing Society is thus based on governing informational propulsions inducing added value and all related information common goods. In other words, the exploratory approach for governing Society relies on information common goods, which are formed from information services and organised as informational commons, in order to establish bases of the progression of Society by means of services. To support the development of services in a sustainable and responsible way, we suggest a protected place adapted to co-construction of information services, called Tiers-Lieu for Services (TLS). To govern them, we should ensure it is done in an exploratory way in co-design, so that responsible and interested persons could all actively participate. This is enabled by people-public-private partnerships for services (4PS), an institutional instrument of the administration of informational propulsions.

3 Service Design Through Tiers-Lieu for Services

Information common goods are formed of information services related to multiple institutions, professions, responsibilities, disciplines. It is thus essential to encourage people who are interested in governing Society, to participate in it by conceiving, creating, implementing them, by mixing various aspects of engineering and exact sciences with aspects of law, management, human sciences, and by continually conducting explorations.

These people will need a protected place, outside of their own institutions, where they can face their differences, sometimes even their divergences, by focusing on co-creating services. A possible candidate for such a protected place is Tiers-Lieu for Services (TLS) [11].

Conceptually, Tiers-Lieu is "a social configuration where the encounter between individual entities intentionally engages in the conception of common representations" [12]. This social configuration is an open place that allows co-creation processes involving various people. It is sufficient to adapt it to the characteristics of informational propulsions and information common goods, in order to make it the place of their construction under the name of Tiers-Lieu for Services: the TLS configuration is a social configuration between different entities whose encounter intentionally engages them in the conception of common informational representations, expressed by means of informational models, in order to construct information services assembling in an information common good.

TLS initiators propose an action corresponding to an informational propulsion of Society. It is described by a pursued intention, with the sense, which it gives to the subsequent progression of Society. It also describes situations to overcome and societal issues of the informational propulsion. This intention leads to defining a corresponding initiative, which is concretised through information. The information plays the key role: it enables the development of multiple propulsions and provides their informational base. This informational base consists of a multitude of informational models, all oriented towards the design and implementation of propulsions. In a generic way, TLS is a social configuration that allows all contributors to have access to informational models of the information service. They can therefore criticize these models. They can make proposals for modifications or even progressions. They can give them the sense in the context of governing Society.

To support the activities of contributors, TLS provides them with a framework: the cross-pollination space [13]. Despite their heterogeneity, they share the common language of the cross-pollination space, the language of information, so they can understand each other and to conceive informational models essential for the implementation of information trans-services. They exchange views and continue explorations by emerging the points of view that are not usual in their own activities, throughout the process of establishing informational models. The informational model is based on the informational base, as well as all the digital and organisational implementations that have been put in place, in order to make operational the information service they are co-designing.

TLS sessions can take many forms: face-to-face or virtual meetings, or their combination. They are all facilitated by a digital platform dedicated to TLS. In all these sessions, there are many innovative ideas that come up and are exploited. TLS takes place under a free license adapted to the constitution of information services and information common goods, following the example of software projects governed by free licenses like the GNU-GPL.

4   4PS

Since there is a huge number of various complex activities and responsibilities related to any informational propulsion, it is essential to have an institutional instrument supporting elaborating and enabling the governance of Society in the context of Smarter Life. This instrument should be designed in the way that all contributors for propulsions can operate efficiently and fully fulfil their responsibilities. This instrument should make it possible to form the necessary partnerships between all physical and legal persons, the world of private or public enterprises, public administrations, associations, national or international organisations, research and training centres, associations of citizens interested in contributing to the co-construction of one or another information service of an informational propulsion. As such an institutional instrument, we suggest to implement 4PS: people-public-private partnerships for services.

4PS is built on the basis of a formal framework, Public-Private Partnerships (PPP), which is well-known internationally and has shown efficiency in various projects. Generally, PPP is defined as a long-term contract between a private party and a government entity, for providing a public asset or service, in which the private party bears significant risk and management responsibility and remuneration is linked to performance [14]. Traditionally, PPP is intended to facilitate public-private partnerships mainly in the context of infrastructure (hospitals, transport, buildings) and is not particularly focused on services. To enable service creation, our exploratory approach suggests to expand PPP to people-public-private partnerships for services (4PS). 4PS does not only benefit from the advantages of PPP that typically allocates each risk to the party that can best manage and handle it, optimises management responsibility and finds coherence between private interests and the public interest. 4PS specifically targets service design and co-creation, where the key role is given to talented persons who actively collaborate in defining, concretising and developing services.

4PS enables the governing of Society to access the design levels of informational propulsions. It can: (i) guarantee the compliance of informational propulsions with regulatory frames; (ii) steer the progression of Society by taking into account the informational propulsions, by fostering their construction, notably by supporting the necessary expansion of regulatory frames (including in some situations the legal frame); (iii) decide the concordance between the construction of informational propulsions and the politics of the progression of Society.

Furthermore, 4PS fosters more inclusive progression that allows active engagement of communities, discloses more information about propulsions, especially on the commitments made to various contributors through the information common goods, and de-risks informational propulsions by providing more predictability in their enabling environment.

5 Conclusion

This exploratory approach with information services, information common goods, TLS and 4PS places constructors of informational propulsions for Smarter Life in more consistent positions, where they can contribute to the progression of Society in concordance with their own competencies and legitimacy. This approach lies on the powerful information level, inherited from IS engineering with its methods, models and techniques. This information level provides a meeting place for persons in charge of governing Society and of constructing information services and informational propulsions in the context of Smarter Life.

References

1. Steffen, W., et al.: Planetary boundaries: guiding human development on a changing planet. Science **347**(6223) (2015). https://science.sciencemag.org/content/347/6223/1259855. Accessed 19 Feb 2020
2. WBGU report, Towards our Common Digital Future. https://www.wbgu.de/en/publications/publication/towards-our-common-digital-future. Accessed 19 Feb 2020
3. SDG. https://sustainabledevelopment.un.org/?menu=1300. Accessed 19 Feb 2020
4. Osburg, Th., Lohrmann, Ch. (eds.): Sustainability in a Digital World: New Opportunities Through New Technologies. Springer Cham (2007). https://www.springer.com/gp/book/9783319546025. Accessed 19 Feb 2020
5. Sachs, J., Schmidt-Traub, G., Kroll, C., Lafortune, G., Fuller, G.: Sustainable Development Report 2019. Bertelsmann Stiftung and Sustainable Development Solutions Network, New York (2019), https://www.sustainabledevelopment.report/. Accessed 19 Feb 2020
6. Armstrong, K.A.: Governing Social Inclusion: Europeanization Through Policy Coordination. Oxford University Press, Oxford (2010)
7. Spohrer, J., Maglio, P.P.: Service science: toward a smarter planet. In: Karwowski, W., Salvendy, G. (eds.) Service Engineering. Wiley, New York (2009)
8. Ostrom, E.: Governing the Commons: The Evolution of Institutions for Collective Action. Political Economy of Institutions and Decisions. Cambridge University Press, Cambridge (1990)
9. Hardin, G.: The tragedy of the commons. Science **162**(3859), 1243–1248 (1968)
10. Yurchyshyna, A.: Towards contributory development by the means of services as common goods. In: Nóvoa, H., Drăgoicea, M. (eds.) IESS 2015. LNBIP, vol. 201, pp. 12–24. Springer, Cham (2015). https://doi.org/10.1007/978-3-319-14980-6_2
11. Ralyté, J., Léonard, M.: Tiers-Lieu for services: an exploratory approach to societal progression. In: Nóvoa, H., Drăgoicea, M., Kühl, N. (eds.) IESS 2020. LNBIP, vol. 377, pp. 289–303. Springer, Cham (2020). https://doi.org/10.1007/978-3-030-38724-2_21
12. Burret, A.: Étude de la configuration en tiers-lieu: la re-politisation par le service. Ph.D. thesis in Sociology and Anthropology, Université des Lumières de Lyon (2017)
13. Léonard, M., Yurchyshyna, A.: Tiers-Lieu: exploratory environments for service-centered innovations. In: Proceedings of the IESS 2013. LNBIP, vol. 143. Springer, Cham (2013)
14. PPP reference guide. https://pppknowledgelab.org/guide/. Accessed 29 Feb 2020

Author Index

Printed in the United States
By Bookmasters